the prideful soul's guide to humility

Thomas Jones and
Michael Fontenot

The Prideful Soul's Guide to Humility.

©2018 by Illumination Publishers, 6010 Pinecreek Ridge Court, Spring, Texas 77379. Available at www.ipibooks.com.

All rights reserved. No part of this book may be duplicated, copied, translated, reproduced or stored mechanically or electronicly without specific written permission of Illumination Publishers.

All Scripture quotations, unless indicated, are taken from the New International Version. Copyright ©1973, 1978, 1984, 2011 by the International Bible Society. Used by permission of Zondervan Publishing House. All rights reserved.

Printed in the United States of America. ISBN: 978-1-948450-26-3.

Cover design by Chris Costello. Additional designs by Toney C. Mulhollan.

About the authors: Mike and Tess Fontenot live in Sydney, Australia where he serves as an elder and evangelist for a church there. They have three daughters and sons-in-law, with ten grandchildren. He also serves as a director of the School of Missions, which trains men and women for Christian ministry.

Tom and Sheila Jones make their home in Nashville, Tennessee. Tom is the author of *No One Like Him: Jesus and His Message* and several other books. He and his wife, Sheila, have both served as writers, editors and are inspirational teachers on various Biblical topics.

Illumination Publishers titles may be purchased in bulk for classroom instruction, teaching seminars, or sales promotional use. For information, please email Paul Vasquez at paul.ipibooks@me.com.

Illumination Publishers cares deeply about using renewable resources and uses recycled paper whenever possible.

From Thomas

To four wonderful women who have made my world much more beautiful—my wife, Sheila, and our three daughters, Amy, Bethany and Corrie.

From Michael

To my incredible wife, Terrie, and my three marvelous daughters, Mandy, Megan and Michelle, who have motivated me toward humility in order to keep my house intact. (Proverbs 15:25)

Contents

Acknowledgments 5
Introduction 7

Part One—HUMILITY AND SPIRITUALITY
1. The Problem with Pride 12
2. The Basis for Humility 18
3. The Humility of Jesus 26
4. Humility and the Cross 31
5. Walk Humbly with Your God
   Part 1: Faith and Prayer 38
6. Walk Humbly with Your God
   Part 2: Obedience and Surrender 46
7. What Humility is Not 54
8. God's Work in Humbling Us 61

Part Two—HUMILITY AND RELATIONSHIPS
9. Humility Toward All People 70
10. Humility in "Discipling" 79
11. Humility and Marriage 85
12. Humility and Parenting 91
13. Humility in Leadership 98
14. Humility and "Followship" 105

Part Three—HUMILITY AND LIFE
15. Humility in Suffering 112
16. Humility and Convictions 119
17. Humility in Success and Failure 129
18. Humility and Talent 134

THE CONCLUSION
19. The Pursuit of Humility 141
20. The Power of Humility 147

APPENDIXES
1. Is Pride Ever Good? 156
2. Classic Expressions of Pride 161
3. Short Thoughts on Humility 165

acknowledgments

The opportunity to write this book together is one for which we are both very grateful. Our friendship began in the fall of 1975 and has continued until now, even though great distances often have separated us for years at a time. We are different characters with different personalities, but there is much we have in common. We both grew up in the Deep South during some of America's most turbulent years. We met in an effort to minister to college students and enjoyed many exciting times during that endeavor. When we had dinner together last year in Jerusalem, it was humbling to talk about how far God had brought us and what he had allowed our eyes to see since our first meeting more than twenty years ago.

God has blessed us both with beautiful, talented and spiritually minded wives and amazingly, with six daughters between us who are very much like their mothers. To this group of eight exceptional women (Terrie, Megan and Michelle Fontenot and Mandy Fontenot Versele, and Sheila, Bethany and Corrie Jones and Amy Jones Black), we acknowledge our deepest appreciation. Without them this book would not have been written.

In addition to our families, we are grateful for the encouragement and input we have received from many special friends. Others from around the world also sent ideas when we first announced to them that this project was underway. Many of those thoughts have influenced this work.

We also want to acknowledge two writers, each of whom "being dead yet speaketh." We have been greatly influenced by the thin volume simply called *Humility* written by Andrew Murray in the nineteenth century and by the work of one of the twentieth century's greatest talents, C. S. Lewis. His little book *Mere Christianity* has a short but powerful section on pride that influenced us both at the beginning of our ministries. Because Murray's work is more thorough on this subject, we will quote from his material on several occasions and perhaps include his ideas unconsciously at other times. His book is a classic. We pray our work will have only something of the enduring quality of his thoughts.

We also want to acknowledge with much appreciation the work of the editorial and design staff of Discipleship Publications International—particularly Kim Hanson, Lisa Morris and Chris Costello. We are also grateful for the careful eye of DPI's outside proofreader, Amy Morgan of Buffalo, New York.

Above all, we acknowledge that our God is greater and better than we can possibly describe. We are grateful he has given us much help in getting this book done. We are more grateful that he has shown us in his Son, Jesus Christ, what humility is all about.

Thomas Jones
Michael Fontenot

Note: The "J" at the beginning of a chapter indicates Thomas Jones is the primary writer. The "F" indicates Michael Fontenot.

introduction

a dangerous thing

Writing a book on humility is a dangerous thing to do. Once your name gets attached to the subject, people will certainly expect to see in your life the trait you are extolling. Our wives will expect it. Our children. Our friends. Those who work under us. Even those who have read the book and then meet us for the first time. But, if we believe in what we are describing here, why should that matter? Shouldn't we want to be held accountable for living out one of our deepest convictions?

We are writing on this topic not because we think we have arrived at some level that qualifies us to write, or because we think we can do a better job than some others. Only one man was totally qualified by character to write on this subject, and he never wrote anything that we know about for sure, save a few words in the dirt before a trembling woman and a gang of self-righteous religious leaders. We are certainly not writing because we think we have humility all figured out or know every important point to make. We write because this topic simply must be written about. If God would have us proclaim anything, he would have us proclaim the rightness and the power of humility. If there is anything he wants to call our attention to and have us think about, it is humility.

Passage after passage in the Scriptures makes it clear that humility is the way to God's heart. The proud find the door closed to his inner sanctum, but those who demonstrate humility are welcomed there again and again. By some measures of performance the former group may outshine the latter, but never mind. God does not receive us on the basis of performance. He receives us on the basis of heart, and no quality of heart is more important to him than humility.

There is nothing more important for a disciple of Jesus than humility. We are not overstating the case to say that we will not be in God's church at all if we do not heartily embrace the message of this book. We are not saying you must get the message from this book or agree with every detail that you find here. But we are saying you must get the message of humility from somewhere, and put it in your heart.

With the Twelve chosen by Jesus wanting to know who would be the greatest in the kingdom of God, Jesus called a little child (*pidion* in Greek—a toddler) and had him stand among them. With twelve proud men looking down at this tiny tot in their midst, Jesus said,

> "I tell you the truth, unless you change and become like little children, you will never enter the kingdom of heaven. Therefore, whoever humbles himself like this child is the greatest in the kingdom of heaven." (Matthew 18:3-4)

Jesus often said things that were designed to get his disciples' attention—to break through their dullness. This was likely one of those times. Jesus' pointed words make it clear that humility is not something to work on *someday*. It is not a secondary quality that is nice to have and one that makes a person a bit easier to get along with. It is the fundamental of all fundamentals. It is what Andrew Murray called "the cardinal virtue" and "the only root from which the graces can grow." It is the queen of all attitudes. It is the soul of discipleship. It is the one attitude of heart and mind that we must be most concerned about. It is the one quality, above all else, for which to pray.

You can be successful with God without being highly intelligent, quick with your wit, clever in business, outstanding in appearance or skillful in athletics (praise God!). *But you cannot be successful with God without humility.* God can work in your life in remarkable ways, even if you do not have great conversation skills, a naturally winsome personality or a quick recall of facts. But remarkably, you will not be in his kingdom at all without humility.

In the early stages of writing this book, I had a discussion about doubt with some young Christians. One was particularly concerned that she still found herself having some doubts after several years of being a Christian. What I told her that day is something I believe deeply: While doubt is sometimes rebuked in the Scriptures, it is not always viewed as a horrible problem. Doubters are not automatically condemned, but are often given help and shown mercy (see Matthew 28:16-20, John 20:21-28, Jude 22). What you have to be most concerned about is pride. If you stay humble as you face your doubts, remaining teachable and open to counsel, you will work them through, and you will be fine.

I further told her that the problem comes when people doubt and become prideful in their doubts. That is a deadly combination. The truth is that you can add pride to any number of challenges and you get the same result. Failure plus humility will lead to eventual victory—example: Peter. Failure plus pride leads to more failure—example: Judas. Add humility to weaknesses, disappointments and the like, and you will eventually get a good outcome. We have all heard that *what happens to us* is not nearly as important as *the attitude that we have* when it happens. This is true, and humility is the most crucial attitude we can ever have.

Most of you who have taken the time to open this book will quickly agree that humility is good and pride is not. Our problem comes, however, in how we rationalize our pride and are blind to our lack of humility. Therefore, in this book we will not just tout the benefits of humility, but our goal will be to see ourselves better and to understand how to truly become humble in the trenches of life.

As we will see, God promises to bless humility. This clearly means it is something he wants us to pursue. The nature of humility, however, is such that we will never be able to stand at its summit, like victorious climbers, and proclaim that we have arrived. The more we pursue it, the more aware we will be that we need it. The reward for this quest never comes in achievement. The reward for pursuing humility is found in the fact that it draws us ever closer to the heart of God—the very place for which we were made.

Abba, Father, God Almighty, as we prepare to look more closely at the meaning of humility, we confess our need for your guidance and the conviction brought about by your Spirit. Our flesh is seldom, if ever, inclined toward true humility. We need a work of your grace to change our hearts, minds and actions. We are grateful you want to help us make such changes, and we come now in expectation of your powerful work. Through Christ we pray, Amen.

part one

humility and spirituality

chapter 1

the problem with pride

> But after Uzziah became powerful, his pride led to his downfall. He was unfaithful to the LORD his God, and entered the temple of the LORD to burn incense on the altar of incense. (2 Chronicles 26:16)
>
> But Hezekiah's heart was proud and he did not respond to the kindness shown him; therefore the Lord's wrath was on him and on Judah and Jerusalem. (2 Chronicles 32:25)

The two kings described in these passages were men who had seen God pour out his blessings. They accomplished much, and they experienced great success because God was with them. One was even healed of a terrible condition. But in both cases pride rose up in their hearts, and pride put them at odds with their God—as it always does. Uzziah and Hezekiah are two distinctively Biblical names, names we should not forget. They are powerful reminders to us of the seriousness, the folly and the utter wastefulness of pride. Because of pride, much that had been gained was thrown away. Much that had been accomplished was completely undone. Hezekiah later repented, and there is hope in that for us all, but you can be sure that had he not repented, God's blessing would not have been restored. Pride is that serious. It is the exact opposite of humility, and God's response to pride is the exact opposite of his response to humility.

What is pride? It is almost always an attitude of self-sufficiency and independence ("I can handle this without help" or "I understand my situation better than anyone else"). It is often an attitude of self-righteousness ("I am at least as good as you are, probably better"). It is sometimes an attitude of boastfulness ("Look what I did, and look what this proves I can do"). It is commonly an attitude of superiority ("My intellect is greater, or my accomplishments are greater, or my looks are greater or something about me is greater"). Pride looks down on others. Pride does not listen well. It is stubborn. Pride is not eager to learn because it is confident in what it already knows. Pride is not quick to admit wrong because it fears it may look bad or lose its position. Pride is competitive and is easily threatened. Pride is insecure. Pride finds it hard to rejoice in the success of others.

The truth is, we are all prideful souls in one way or another. In different personalities, pride shows itself in different ways, but it is in us all. People are sometimes fooled because their pride may not be the "in your face," arrogant type, but if they do not have a deep humility before God and before people, pride is hiding somewhere in the folds of the personality; spiritual victory cannot be gained until the pride is revealed and put to death.

Our biggest problem, however, is not found in admitting we have pride. Our biggest problem lies in taking it seriously. Far too many Christians still take pride too lightly. In fact, it is not uncommon to hear those in leadership roles joke about their pride. "I know, I know, I'm just a prideful dog," quips a speaker as he tells a story about an interaction between his wife and himself. The audience laughs, just as he intended for them to do. But would we joke about any other sin in the same way? Imagine a speaker who says, "I know, I know, I'm just an adulterous man," expecting the audience to laugh. Or imagine someone saying, "I'm just a stinking child abuser," thinking that he will endear himself to his hearers. It is to Satan's credit how we have taken the sin that is the deepest and the most serious and have minimized and trivialized it. Before we will make much progress in becoming truly humble before God and each other, we must see the seriousness of our pride.

The Great Sin

What quality is most detested by God? What attitude of heart will always bring about a downfall? What character trait will ensure that there will be division? What quality cannot co-exist with love? Pride is the answer in each case, and that is quite a list. These are not the conclusions of modern moral philosophers. These are the clear statements of Scripture. When C. S. Lewis called pride the "Great Sin," he could not have been on firmer Biblical ground. It can be argued that there is no sin that is not somehow rooted in pride. Consider a few examples:

- Sexual immorality: "I deserve to have my pleasure, and I should not have to worry about consequences."
- Lying: "I do not trust that God can work through the truth. I have more confidence in my ability to deceive and to distort the facts."
- Hatred: "I am better than you are, and I have a right to despise you for what you have done or what you are."
- Rebellion: "I know better than my leaders, and I can accomplish better things by doing what I want to do."
- Ignoring the needs of others: "My life is the most important thing: accomplishing my goals, getting my pleasure, fulfilling my needs."
- Ingratitude: "I have what I have because I worked for it, or at least because I deserve it. Plus, there are other things that I deserve to have."
- Disobedience: "I know the Bible says this, but I have a better way."
- Discord: "I have no need for a relationship with you. I will be able to accomplish what I need to without unity."
- Prejudice and racism: "Those people just aren't as good as we are."

This list is not complete, but it does remind us that pride is at the heart of all sin. It is a fundamental quality that is often down below the surface, but one that we must root out and expose if we are to have a close walk with God.

Pride is deadly serious because it keeps us from seeing our tremendous need for God. Where there is pride, there is no spirit of utter dependence on him. The psalmist surely had this in mind when he wrote:

> In his pride the wicked does not seek him;
> in all his thoughts there is no room for God.
> (Psalm 10:4)

In Proverbs 8:13 wisdom says:

> To fear the Lord is to hate evil;
> I [wisdom] hate pride and arrogance,
> evil behavior and perverse speech. (Proverbs 8:13)

When wisdom speaks in Proverbs, it is clearly God who is speaking. The God who hates a lying tongue and those who shed innocent blood (Proverbs 6:16-17) also hates pride and arrogance. We would not joke about the killing of innocents. Should we make light of pride?

God takes no delight in the punishment of any man (Ezekiel 18:32), yet the prideful soul must be dealt with because it is so set against God:

> The Lord detests all the proud of heart.
> Be sure of this: They will not go unpunished.
> (Proverbs 16:5)

Both James and Peter quote from the Old Testament and remind us that "God opposes the proud but gives grace to the humble" (James 4:6, 1 Peter 5:5). That one statement is more than enough to cause us to see pride as a wicked, ugly thing. We cannot see it as a benign annoyance or a lovable flaw, but as a trait of the sinful nature that must be put to death.

What a Waste!

There are an abundance of Biblical reasons for taking pride seriously and for setting ourselves against it. But let us call attention to one in particular: *Pride is so wasteful.* So much time is wasted because of pride. So much money and energy is wasted because of it. Those of us in God's kingdom have a divine mission, and we have limited amounts of time, money and energy to carry it out. But how many of these valuable resources are wasted simply because of how stubborn, resistant and prideful we can be?

We see reports in the media on how much alcoholism costs our society. There are the costs associated with the injuries and deaths caused by those who drink and drive. There are the missed days of work. There are the hospitalizations. There is the money spent arresting, jailing and prosecuting drunk drivers. There is the higher cost of auto and health insurance. We look at all that and say, "What a waste! All that money could be used for better things."

In the same way, we need to look at all the hours that are spent simply because we are holding onto our pride. We need to look personally at how much time we have required of others for that very reason. What a waste! Both of us who are writing can think of numerous situations when Christians could have been using an evening to find someone new to bring to Christ. Instead, those hours were spent trying to get some fellow Christian who knew better to let go of their pride and just let God work. There is really no way to estimate how many hours could have been used for fresh impact on a waiting world that were instead spent trying to convince a prideful Christian of something that humility would have grasped in a moment.

Pride is a nasty thing. Pride is as wicked as it gets. Pride hurts. Pride wastes. Ultimately, pride kills. In this book our focus will be on humility. We will extol its power. We will show how it can become more and more the heart of our lives. In the process, however, we will have to return often to the issue of pride, for it is only as pride dies that humility can live.

▪ Thought Question ▪
What evidence is there that you take seriously the sin of pride in your life?

chapter 2

the basis for humility

Humility in our world is rare. In some ways this is not surprising. Nothing comes to us more naturally than pride. Our instinct is to think first of ourselves (at least until we become mothers or fathers). If winners are being announced for awards, we are more focused on ourselves than on our friends. We hear a speaker describing people in the audience that he or she appreciates, and if that speaker knows us, we wait to hear our names mentioned. If that doesn't happen, we wonder why. Someone shows us a group photo that includes us, and we immediately check to see how we look. I am coauthoring this book with one of my best friends in the world. However, when the book is released, sadly, my first instinct will be to reread *my* chapters, to see how they look, and only later to look again at his. (Having been honest about this hopefully will help me act differently.)

It is not surprising that humility is rare, because it does not come naturally. However, in another way, it is rather odd, for nothing is more reasonable and logical and sensible than humility. Conversely, nothing is more foolish than pride.

All Pride Is Groundless

When the famous Charles Spurgeon preached about pride, his first point was that pride is such a *groundless* thing. With his characteristic eloquence Spurgeon said:

Pride stands on the sands; or worse than that, it puts its foot on the billows which yield beneath its tread; or worse still, it stands on bubbles, which soon must burst beneath its feet. Of all things pride has the worst foothold; it has no solid rock on earth whereon to place itself. We have reasons for almost everything, but we have no reasons for pride. Pride is a thing which should be unnatural to us, for we have nothing to be proud of.[1]

Words well spoken. People will sometimes be very prideful about their heritage or their ancestry or their race, when they had absolutely nothing to do with the fact that they ended up in a certain family. People are often prideful about accomplishments, while in every case they were dependent on someone else in some way for those. Nobody ever got through the first year of life—or even the first several years of life—without someone meeting needs that they could not possibly have met on their own. Even in those rare cases when a child was abandoned by a mother, someone stepped in and provided.

"No man is an island; no man stands alone," said the song from the 1960s, echoing the words penned three hundred years earlier by poet John Donne. No one has done it, whatever *it* is, entirely on his or her own. The star athlete, the Wall Street billionaire, the famous author, the Oscar-winning actor, the Olympic champion, the star attorney, the guy you know who just built a fabulous new home—they all have one thing in common: Other people contributed to their success. They need to be grateful for and humble about the help they have received.

Humility Fits with Reality

But as important as this is, there is a much deeper reason for humility. Already we have begun to approach this reason, but we need to grasp it completely. Humility is so right because it so squares with reality. It is a reality that we owe other people a great deal. Now consider an even deeper reality: *There is a*

*God, and you are not him.*² There is a great and an awesome God who created the heavens and the earth, and you are not him. There is a God who knows all and understands all and is in control of all, and you are not him. And I am not him. He is God, and we are not. He is the great God, and you and I are small people—very small in comparison to him!

Some people don't like this. But what they like or don't like does not change reality. When one of our children was small, she did not like it that she was small. She also did not like that we were bigger and stronger and could make her do what she did not want to do. She had intense feelings about this, but likes and dislikes did not change a thing. We stayed big, and at least for a few years, she stayed small. There have been plenty of children who thought the way she thought. (Some of you may have one like that in the next room!) But a million children thinking this way would not change a thing. They would still be small, and their parents would still be able to make them go to bed and tell them when it is time to come in at night.

It is the same with us in our relationship to God. From the beginning man has had problems with the fact that he is not God. In fact, all of man's problems stem from the fact that he wants to be like God and wants to have the knowledge and the power that God has. But none of that has ever changed reality. God is still God and man is still *not* God. The Psalmist described reality:

> From heaven the LORD looks down
> and sees all mankind;
> from his dwelling place he watches
> all who live on earth. (Psalm 33:13-14)

God is in heaven. Man is on earth. God is above us. He is higher than we are. He is greater than we are. He can see what we cannot see. It is accurate to say he "looks down" on us, for that is the only way in the normal state of things that he can look at us. His ways are higher than our ways. His perspective is vastly broader than ours. His ability is infinitely beyond ours. He looks down and we must look up. I know several people who are almost seven feet tall. The reality is that when we stand together, they look down on me. They are not being prideful or condescending. It is just that it is more than twelve inches from their eyes down to mine. The reality of the situation requires me to look up.

In the same way God is higher than we are, and the difference between God and us is a lot more than a foot (a lot more than any physical distance!). The reality is that we share the Cosmos with a great and awesome God (because of his grace, by the way), and for that reason, humility makes all the sense in the world. For the same reason, pride is groundless and ridiculous. The next time you are tempted with pride, sit under the starry heavens, contemplate the vastness of the universe and let God ask you some of the questions that he asked Job:

> "Where were you when I laid the earth's foundation?
>   Tell me, if you understand." (Job 38:4)
>
> "Have you ever given orders to the morning,
>   or shown the dawn its place?" (Job 38:12)
>
> "Do you send the lightning bolts on their way?
>   Do they report to you, 'Here we are'?" (Job 38:35)
>
> "Does the hawk take flight by your wisdom
>   and spread his wings toward the south?" (Job 39:26)

Perhaps the contemplation of such questions will bring us back to our senses as Job was brought back to his. Hear the beginning of his reply:

> "I am unworthy—how can I reply to you?
>   I put my hand over my mouth.
> I spoke once, but I have no answer—
>   twice, but I will say no more." (Job 40:4-5)

Reality Will Not Change

Man will never succeed in his effort to pull himself up to the level of God, and he certainly will never be in a position where he will be able to look down on God. Cocky, arrogant man may make disparaging comments about God. He may ridicule God. He may prance and strut around as though he is more clever than God. He may boast that he does not need God. He may live as though he is "the master of his fate and the captain of his soul." But one day he will stand in the presence of the righteous and holy God, and he will tremble as he realizes that he was never greater than God. It was all an absurd, fool-hearted and deadly game of pretending. Isaiah describes such a man:

> How you have fallen from heaven,
>   O morning star, son of the dawn!
> You have been cast down to the earth,
>   you who once laid low the nations!
> You said in your heart,
>   "I will ascend to heaven;
> I will raise my throne
>   above the stars of God;
> I will sit enthroned on the mount of assembly,
>   on the utmost heights of the sacred mountain.
> I will ascend above the tops of the clouds;
>   I will make myself like the Most High."
> But you are brought down to the grave,
>   to the depths of the pit.
>
> Those who see you stare at you,
>   they ponder your fate:
> "Is this the man who shook the earth
>   and made kingdoms tremble,
> the man who made the world a desert,
>   who overthrew its cities
> and would not let his captives go home?"
> (Isaiah 14:12-17)

This ruler that Isaiah is describing once exercised authority over many. So expansive was his power that he fantasized that he could make himself like the Most High. But his glory was short-lived, and he ended up just like other men in the shame of the grave. He who once intimidated others became the object of men's stares and speculations. So it will be with every prideful soul that does not bow in humility before the God who made him. Nothing man can do will change reality. He is not God. He will never be God. As long as he ignores that truth, his life will be headed for a disastrous conclusion. For God opposes the proud. (Again, see James 4:6 and 1 Peter 5:5.)

The Truth Sets You Free

Jesus taught, "You shall know the truth and the truth will set you free." Even those who do not acknowledge Jesus as the Christ agree that this is the highest kind of wisdom. Universities place this saying over their doors. Scientists are fiercely committed to finding the truth. Whenever you ask for guidance or counsel, you want to get it from someone who is fully in touch with the truth. You would not be interested in going on safari with a guide who believed that with just a little extra effort you could outrun a lion or a rhino. You would want a guide fully in touch with the truth, a guide who knows the limitations of human beings and the amazing strength and speed of those in the animal kingdom.

When you make decisions on the most important issues in your life, you need to be in touch with the most central truths of life. The most important truth any of us can ever know is that there is a God, but we are not him. Any confusion about either one of those things gets us into big trouble. There is a great and powerful God who wants a relationship with us and who will use his amazing power to bless our lives, but we are the creatures and he is the Creator. Everything we have, we have from his hand. Have you done some great things? Have you received some recognition for accomplishments? If so, you did those things with the mind and strength God gave you. Without him you would be nothing. As Paul said to the proud Athenians: "He himself gives all men life and breath and everything else" (Acts 17:25).

My life is full of relationships that are good and work that is fulfilling. I could act as though I have these things because I have worked hard and made some good decisions. That would be foolish. The truth is, everything I have, I have because God made it possible. He is the Alpha and the Omega. He is the beginning and the end. It is all about him from start to finish.

The basis for humility, then, is quite simple. Humility is the only thing that makes sense because of how eternal and unchanging and powerful God is and how fading and precarious and dependent we are. Nothing you do in your life will ever change that. People are sometimes humble until they enjoy some great success. What fools we can be! A little success, achieved by the grace of God, does not change the nature of reality. It does not change who you are and who God is.

Have you noticed how certain people will change their whole attitude depending on whom they are with? Normally, they are cocky and arrogant, maybe even abusive. But when someone much more important or someone who has influence over their paycheck walks in, suddenly they become kind and humble and self-effacing. To live in accordance with the truth, we all need to practice the presence of God. We need to live all the time just as if we were standing in the presence of someone very important—because we are. Think of some recent prideful thing you did. Would you have done that if you had been aware that you were standing in the very presence of the holy, righteous and almighty God? Would you have treated your friend the way you did? Would you have treated your spouse the way you did? Would you have taken the credit that you took? Would you have been defensive when corrected?

It is time for us to face up to reality—the reality of God, and to embrace the truth about God with joy. The result will be a deep and unshakable humility.

• **Thought Question** •

*How does your view of God keep you humble
in all circumstances?*

NOTES

[1] From a sermon delivered on August 17, 1856, by C. H. Spurgeon at New Park Street Chapel.
[2] Apologies to all grammarians, but "you are not he" sounds too strange for me to use, particularly when it is repeated four or five times!

chapter 3

the humility of Jesus

There are not too many people who could describe themselves as humble and have a great number of others believe them. But Jesus did just that. Listen to his words:

> "Come to me, all you who are weary and burdened, and I will give you rest. Take my yoke upon you and learn from me, for I am gentle and humble in heart, and you will find rest for your souls. For my yoke is easy and my burden is light." (Matthew 11:28)

"Learn from me," says Jesus. "Follow me." "Be like me, and you will find rest for your souls." And what specifically does he want us to imitate in his character? In this passage it is his gentleness and his humility. A close look at Jesus' life reveals that this statement was not a hollow claim.

Dependent on God

Jesus understood that he was sent by God, and he did not believe for a moment that he was self-sufficient. Jesus repeatedly used the phrase "who sent me," whether he was speaking to his disciples, to the Jewish leaders or to the masses. Looking in the gospel of John, we can see how totally aware Jesus was of his dependence on God:

> "My food," said Jesus, "is to do the will of him who sent me and to finish his work." (John 4:34)

> "By myself I can do nothing; I judge only as I hear, and my judgment is just, for I seek not to please myself but him who sent me." (John 5:30)

> "For I have come down from heaven not to do my will but to do the will of him who sent me." (John 6:38)

> "For I did not speak of my own accord, but the Father who sent me commanded me what to say and how to say it. I know that his command leads to eternal life. So whatever I say is just what the Father has told me to say." (John 12:49-50)

Jesus did not do or say anything apart from what his Father desired; he was totally dependent on him. At the heart of being humble is being dependent on God. Jesus was the most humble man ever to live, because no one was ever more dependent on God than he was. No one was ever less self-sufficient than the man who seemingly had the most reason to be so.

One of the subtle manifestations of pride is having a self-sufficient attitude. While I don't personally walk around feeling prideful, I do often see an attitude of self-sufficiency in me, which is clearly pride. For example, I like to work alone. I insisted on doing my own work exclusively as I was growing up. I rarely asked for help. I seldom felt lonely, and my escapist dreams were all about being off alone as a farmer or rancher, building something all by myself. Whether it was for school or any other project, I liked to figure it out myself. I thought, "Just give me the book, and I'll work it out." I was even resentful of someone telling me how to do it and irritated as they tried to help me. As a result, I produced mediocrity. My approach would work, but it would be sloppy or inefficient. And the bigger the project, the more the mediocrity would show. So the projects or work became all the more burdensome and wearisome to me.

Pride does not ask for, or like to ask for, help. Whether the goal is to have a better family, a better marriage, to be better in the workplace, to have better relationships, or to be more effective evangelistically, pride guts it out and works it out in that singular arena, totally dependent on self. Pride is in total contrast to Jesus. Jesus is humble in heart and sees his need for God. He did nothing, said nothing apart from his dependence on God. And as a result, Jesus was not weary or burdened with life.

We can be self-sufficient (and therefore prideful) in our efforts to be spiritual. We can be self-reliant in trying to overcome sin. Consider this passage from 2 Chronicles 7:13-14:

> "When I shut up the heavens so that there is no rain, or command locusts to devour the land or send a plague among my people, if my people, who are called by my name, will humble themselves and pray and seek my face and turn from their wicked ways, then will I hear from heaven and will forgive their sin and will heal their land."

Sometimes in Scripture the order of things is very important, and this seems true here. The first step in getting right with God is being humble, *not* "turning from our wicked ways." Now, if we are humble, we do turn. But we should not start by thinking, "I'll turn from my sins, my wicked ways, and then I (in my self-sufficient way) will have earned my place with God. Then I will be humble." Humble is the last thing we will be!

Remembering that we "were bought at a price" (1 Corinthians 6:20) and understanding that we now belong to God helps us to see that we can no longer be self-sufficient. Because God "sends me," my life will change: I will not do what I want, but what God wants, in every area of my life. Jesus was one in essence with God, but his dependence on the Father shows us the heart of humility.

Selfless Servant

Jesus also shows his humility in the way he served. He served others instead of being self-occupied, even in his times of greatest personal trial. No place is this better demonstrated than at the Last Supper with his disciples. As they began to bicker about who was greatest, Jesus took them to task:

> "For who is greater, the one who is at the table or the one who serves? Is it not the one who is at the table? But I am among you as one who serves." (Luke 22:27)

For the disciples, this message about serving was not a new revelation. It was not yet their conviction, but Jesus had been working to get them to see this all along. Throughout his ministry they knew he was "among them as one who serves."

We find in John 13:12-17 the powerful account of Jesus washing his disciples' feet and specifically commanding them to do likewise. Jesus' relationships and interactions were amazing. His disciples, referred to in Acts 4 as "unschooled, ordinary men," are not the types one envisions as associates of the prideful. Jesus welcomed children, women, "sinners," tax collectors, the hurting (lepers, sick) and demoniacs—again, not the associates of the prideful. But Jesus did not just associate with these people, he served them.

I find it amazing that so little is said in the Gospels about ups and downs in Jesus' emotions. But then I think about how serving always pulls me up out of my moodiness, and I think that Jesus may well have avoided the emotional lows because he was always focused on service.

There are several telltale signs of self-occupation: Are your prayers mainly about yourself? Are your conversations mainly about yourself? Do you do most of the talking in your interaction with others? Do you rarely serve others in the mundane ways? Are there some things that you just do not feel you should ever be asked to do? Are you more worried about your position in the eyes of others or in God's eyes? If you are a disciple of Jesus, you will not be afraid of humble service. You will see in his life the glory of service, and you will be ready to take the towel and the basin and wash feet.

Pride offends God by self-exaltation, offends others by self-occupation and damages self by self-deception. This delusion increases until one fancies oneself so high as to be invulnerable. The Bible says a lot about that. Jesus is the opposite at every point.

The appeal we find in the Letters for us to live a different life always traces back to the humility of Jesus:

> By the meekness and gentleness of Christ, I appeal to you.... (2 Corinthians 10:1)

> Do nothing out of selfish ambition or vain conceit, but in humility consider others better than yourselves. Each of you should look not only to your own interests, but also to the interests of others. Your attitude should be the same as that of Christ Jesus. (Philippians 2:3-5)

Disciples of Jesus must have the greatest commitment to humility. Nothing was deeper in his character. His humility is meant to move us, teach us and change us. His was the ultimate example of a life lived for others through the strength of a powerful relationship with God.

▪ Thought Question ▪

What do you see in Jesus' humility that challenges you most?

chapter 4

humility and the cross

This is not just a book about humility. It is a book about the Christian approach to humility. For this reason, we are compelled to include an examination of what Jesus says about taking up the cross and what was involved when he took up his cross. The message of Jesus is not just another moral philosophy that blends blandly in with those of other teachers of ethics. His is a unique message with a shocking, and even offensive, center. At the heart of his teaching there was what Paul would later call "the message of the cross." This word of the cross, Paul would go on to say, is "foolishness to those who are perishing, but to us who are being saved it is the power of God" (1 Corinthians 1:18).

There are dozens of "enlightened" forms of Christianity around today that have virtually expunged the cross from their message. It may still be found atop their steeples, but it is seldom preached from their pulpits. This is nothing new. Reading between the lines, it seems likely that the first-century Corinthian Christians, under the heavy influence of Greek philosophy, with its home just a few miles away in Athens, were becoming embarrassed by the cross. It seems that they were seeking another expression of faith that would soften the emphasis on the cross and be more appealing to their philosophically sophisticated culture. To them Paul affirms that the cross must stay at the very center of our lives and our faith, and he reminds them, "For I resolved to know nothing while I was with you except Jesus Christ and him crucified" (1 Corinthians 2:2).

And so when we come to the subject of humility, we will not really understand it apart from the message of the cross. Nothing teaches us as much about life as the cross of Christ. And nothing teaches us more about humility than the cross.

Even Death on a Cross

When writing to the Philippian church, wanting them to understand how crucial it was that they conduct their relationships with humility, Paul focused their attention on the attitude of Jesus. These often-quoted words need to be freshly examined in view of our subject:

> Do nothing out of selfish ambition or vain conceit, but in humility consider others better than yourselves. Each of you should look not only to your own interests, but also to the interests of others.
>
> Your attitude should be the same as that of Christ Jesus:
>
> Who, being in very nature God,
>   did not consider equality with God something
>   to be grasped,
> but made himself nothing,
>   taking the very nature of a servant,
>   being made in human likeness.
> And being found in appearance as a man,
>   he humbled himself
>   and became obedient to death—
>   even death on a cross! (Philippians 2:3-8)

Christians are not wanting when it comes to a role model. We clearly understand who we are to be like. In our relationships with each other we are to have the same attitude as that which we see in Jesus Christ. In the last chapter we saw specific evidence of Jesus' humility. In this passage Paul shows us how far that humility was willing to go.

First, the one who was in his very nature—in his very essence—God, did not protectively or selfishly grasp or guard those privileges of deity. Instead, the Greek text more accurately could be translated, he "emptied himself" (*keneo*) and became, in his very essence, a servant. From the essence of God to the essence of a servant. This text is showing us that the God of the universe is in his essence humble—a remarkable truth available to us only through revelation. (Human reasoning and speculative philosophy could never have come to such a conclusion.)

But Paul is not through. Jesus not only took the nature of a servant, but "he humbled himself and became obedient to death—even death on a cross!" "Even death on a cross." Perhaps we have heard those words too many times to appreciate the original impact. Crosses were despised. Death on a cross brought a humiliation worse than any other. Crucifixion was often used for the death of a rebellious and useless slave. It was a form of execution invented by the Persians and perfected by the Romans. Roman law guaranteed that no Roman citizen would ever have to die this way, no matter how heinous his crime. And so the Son of God came and died a type of death that no citizen of the empire would ever have to die. And yet he was innocent, not only of any crime against society, but even of the "smallest" of sins.

"Even death on a cross." The message of the cross teaches us many things. At the top of the list is how wide and long and deep and high is the love of God. There is nothing he would not do to save us. Sin was this bad. The only way to deal with it was for him to go this far. (Given the account in Luke 22:41-46, we can be sure of this.) But God is selfless and humble, and his humility knows no bounds. Jesus did not draw a line and say, "This far, but no farther." Some of us may fear humility because we know we will only be willing to go so far. Not Jesus. He was not concerned about protecting his image—only about saving lost people. What a lesson we need to learn from that!

In Jesus' action we also learn something powerful about how humility stands in awe of God. The Scripture says, "He humbled himself and *became obedient*, even to death on a cross"

(Philippians 2:8, emphasis added). His was a lifetime of obedience to his Father, but it was obedience even to death on a cross. He was in such awe of his Father that his heart stayed obedient, even when the call was to something painful, humiliating and distasteful, but needed. Disobedience was not an option for him. He prayed and prayed until he was able to obey. On the other hand, some of us do not like to obey anyone at any time. We do not mind doing something as long as it is entirely our idea, but as soon as it becomes a matter of obedience, we resist. We do not have the awe for God that Jesus had. We are still affected by a pride that was not found in the heart of Jesus.

Follow Me

The message of Philippians 2 tells us a great deal about Jesus, but Paul did not write it just for that purpose. What we find in Jesus is there to train us:

> Do nothing out of selfish ambition or vain conceit, but in humility consider others better than yourselves. Each of you should look not only to your own interests, but also to the interests of others.
>
> Your attitude should be the same as that of Christ Jesus.

A more literal rendering of that last verse would be: "Have in you this mind that was in Christ Jesus." We need to think the same way Jesus did. We need to see at the cross how dramatically and deeply humble he was, but then we need to be like him in our relationship with God and in our relationships with others.

Before he literally went to the cross, Jesus was teaching his disciples that his was a crucified lifestyle and that they could only follow him if they took up the cross.

> "...and anyone who does not take his cross and follow me is not worthy of me." (Matthew 10:38)

> Then he said to them all: "If anyone would come after me, he must deny himself and take up his cross daily and follow me." (Luke 9:23)
>
> "And anyone who does not carry his cross and follow me cannot be my disciple." (Luke 14:27)

The passage in Luke 9 and the parallel passages in Matthew 16 and Mark 8 show plainly that taking up the cross is linked with a denial of self. Jesus is describing an approach to life in which we take the unusual step of denying self and then put that disowned self on the cross for a daily death. This passage is the heart of Jesus' message, which shows the drastic difference between Jesus' and the world's philosophy. This, too, is the message of the cross that is foolishness to those who are perishing.

Our training in the secular world teaches us to protect self, to defend it, to guard its rights, even to tastefully tout its accomplishments. God's wisdom is entirely different. Jesus calls us to lose our lives and promises that when we lose them for him and for the gospel, we will find them.

It is not hard to see how this fits with humility. The man who is dying to himself will not pridefully defend his sin. He will be grateful for those who help him see it; he will decide to confess it and expose it, being confident that this will lead to encouragement for all around him.

The woman who says "I am crucified with Christ; I no longer live, but Christ lives in me" will not be trying to prove to you how she does not need advice. She realizes that she has died (and continues to die) to her need to look competent and worthy of praise. She gives up her desire to be right and to impress others with her intelligence, wisdom or savvy. She now focuses on what will most draw attention to Jesus and what will most advance his kingdom on earth.

The disciple of Jesus who is taking up his cross and getting on it, will not be looking down upon other Christians who are not where he is spiritually. The cross of Christ will be too much on his mind to compare himself with others. He will be keenly aware of his sin, for which Christ died, including the sinful pride in his own heart that daily needs to be crucified. For him, the ground at the foot of the cross will indeed be level. If he does any comparing, it will be to see others, in humility, as better than himself (back to Philippians 2:3).

The Christian who wants the mind of Christ will realize that the first thing that needs to be crucified every day is his pride. It was not found in Jesus at all, and nothing will keep us from finding the power of God more than our pride. In John's gospel Jesus' message about his death and our dying to self reads like this:

> "I tell you the truth, unless a kernel of wheat falls to the ground and dies, it remains only a single seed. But if it dies, it produces many seeds." (John 12:24)

When we die with Christ, when we go to the cross, it is not a meaningless death. Our death to self produces many seeds (some translations say "much fruit"), and certainly one of the chief fruits produced will be humility. Such humility then paves the way for God to use us powerfully in all kinds of situations.

The message of the cross was foolishness to the world; it still is and it always will be. But to us who embrace it, that message will always be the wisdom and power of God. It will produce in us the humility we can never generate through self-discipline. It will change the way we relate to God and the way we treat others. We can be sure that we never would have figured out the power of humility on our own, but we can thank God for him who was willing to take the form of a servant, humble himself and become obedient *even to death on a cross* and thus, show us how to live!

▪ **Thought Question** ▪

When was the last time you made a conscious decision to crucify your pride?

chapter 5

walk humbly with your God
Part 1: Faith and Prayer

> He has showed you, O man, what is good.
>   And what does the Lord require of you?
> To act justly and to love mercy
>   and to walk humbly with your God.
> Micah 6:8

There is no true humility that is not rooted in a relationship with God, and there is no relationship with God without humility. It is rare to find a person who appears to be a humble man or woman who does not walk with God. In fact if you find such a person, you will often see just how lacking they are in true humility when you confront them with the word of God. Many a prideful soul has been exposed by its reaction to the truth of Scripture. The person who had appeared to be gentle and humble turns out to be angry and bitter, or at least very independent and self-reliant, when shown how God calls for change in his life.

People who do not focus on God cannot be truly and thoroughly humble. A man or woman may not be annoyingly arrogant, but without reverence for God, it is only a matter of time until pride will be manifest in them in some fashion in some relationship. It is only before the awesomeness of God and his equally awesome generosity and grace that we understand what humility is all about. Unless a person consistently stands in awe of God, his humility will be shallow and easily replaced by pride.

On the other hand, it is also true that we will have no ongoing and growing relationship with God without a consistently humble posture in our relationship with him. Many a soul has come to God and humbly accepted his message only to later grow proud again. We are a fickle people. Our hearts wax and wane. The warning given in Deuteronomy to the Israelites is still needed today:

> Be careful that you do not forget the Lord your God, failing to observe his commands, his laws and his decrees that I am giving you this day. Otherwise, when you eat and are satisfied, when you build fine houses and settle down, and when your herds and flocks grow large and your silver and gold increase and all you have is multiplied, then your heart will become proud and you will forget the Lord your God, who brought you out of Egypt, out of the land of slavery. (Deuteronomy 8:11-14)

In God's church in our day, there are people who came to him originally with childlike humility and a sense of wonder, but success, or in some cases painful circumstances and disappointments, have caused them to become prideful. If they are to stay with God, they must return to those qualities they had initially in their walk with him. Humility is an *absolute* requirement for the entire journey, and in this chapter and the next we will see how humility is intimately linked to four vital elements in our relationship with God.

Humility and Faith

Even a cursory reading of the Gospels shows us that Jesus was moved by faith. We can even say that he was exhilarated by finding faith in others. Look at just three examples:

> When Jesus heard this, he was astonished and said to those following him, "I tell you the truth, I have not found anyone in Israel with such great faith." (Matthew 8:10)

> Some men brought to him a paralytic, lying on a mat. When Jesus saw their faith, he said to the paralytic, "Take heart, son; your sins are forgiven." (Matthew 9:2)
>
> Jesus turned and saw her. "Take heart, daughter," he said, "your faith has healed you." And the woman was healed from that moment. (Matthew 9:22)

These and other passages show us that nothing grabs the heart of God like faith. Astonishing Jesus is no small feat. (How do you impress him who made the universe?!) But when Jesus saw the centurion's faith, he was astonished. He was amazed, and he was thrilled to act on this man's behalf. True faith is rare, and God never misses it. His radar scans the earth for it, and he jumps to the aid of those who have it. But what does humility have to do with faith? Much indeed.

Andrew Murray writes, "...we can never have more true faith than we have humility."* His point seems to be reinforced by the three encounters with Jesus we have just considered. In all cases the humility of the people is as evident as their faith. Conversely, the people who never show this kind of faith are the same ones who are not humble (consider the Pharisees, the scribes and Pilate).

When we take steps away from humility, we are pulling up faith by the roots. Intellectual belief in God or in Biblical ideas is useless without humility. The religious leaders of Jesus' day were men with definite beliefs, but Jesus was never amazed at their faith. No, instead he was distressed at their stubborn hearts (Mark 3:5). For the most part they had long since stopped having the humble attitude of a Samuel who said, "Speak, Lord, for your servant is listening" (1 Samuel 3:9). They did a lot of speaking to God, but very little listening to him.

We must not be so prideful as to think that the same thing could not happen to us. By the latter part of the first century, it was already happening to Christians. It was not just a Jewish problem. Look at Revelation 3:17:

> "You say, 'I am rich; I have acquired wealth and do not need a thing.' But you do not realize that you are wretched, pitiful, poor, blind and naked."

The Christians in Laodicea, for whatever reason, had become proud and self-sufficient. They had not left the church. In their own eyes they still had faith. But they were no longer humble before Jesus, and he was just about to leave them (literally "vomit them out," verse 16). If it could happen to Christians under apostolic leadership, you can be sure it can happen to us. In fact it has happened to some of us.

We no longer pray as the publican did, "God, be merciful to me, a sinner." We do not see ourselves as wretched, pitiful, poor, blind and naked. We live in nice places, wear nice clothes and drive nice cars. We put healthy checks in the church offering. We volunteer to help the right projects. We give to others. We don't need a thing. *And we are not listening to a thing.* We have been around for ten or fifteen years, and we think we have heard all there is to hear. We no longer go to church with a heart that says, "Speak, Lord, for your servant is listening and wanting to change." We still believe all the right doctrines. We can teach them to others, but we do not have a living faith that springs from a heart that says, "Lord, just do anything you want to do with me. Show me my heart. Keep me here. Take me there. Just use me in whatever way pleases you."

But there is good news. While the sight of prideful Christians in Laodicea nauseated Jesus, he still was full of grace and offered forgiveness, fellowship and great victory to those who would repent:

> "Those whom I love I rebuke and discipline. So be earnest, and repent. Here I am! I stand at the door and knock. If anyone hears my voice and opens the door, I will come in and eat with him, and he with me.
>
> To him who overcomes, I will give the right to sit with me on my throne, just as I overcame and sat down with my

Father on his throne. He who has an ear, let him hear what the Spirit says to the churches." (Revelation 3:19-22)

The call to repentance that comes from God is full of hope and possibilities because it means that God believes we can still change and that his grace is still available to help us do it. Our faith can be renewed. It can still move mountains. It can still be the victory that overcomes the world. But a revitalized faith always starts with a humble and contrite heart before God. If Jesus would not be amazed at your faith, check your humility level.

Humility and Prayer

During the fifth century B.C., Nehemiah (a Jew living in Persia as a result of the exile from Israel) heard news of the conditions back in Jerusalem. He heard that the wall of Jerusalem was broken down and its gates had been burned. Here are his own words:

> When I heard these things, I sat down and wept. For some days I mourned and fasted and prayed before the God of heaven. Then I said:
>
> > "O LORD, God of heaven, the great and awesome God, who keeps his covenant of love with those who love him and obey his commands, let your ear be attentive and your eyes open to hear the prayer your servant is praying before you day and night for your servants, the people of Israel. I confess the sins we Israelites, including myself and my father's house, have committed against you." (Nehemiah 1:4-6)

Humbled by what he heard, Nehemiah did what humble people do: He prayed. He prayed with passion. He prayed with conviction. He prayed with faith. And God heard him and answered him.

You will never find a humble person who does not pray frequently, fervently and faithfully. A man's prayer life is the barometer of his humility. Find a man who prays little, prays in rote fashion or prays to check something off a list, and you have found a man who is not humble before the great and awesome God.

All humble people know there is a great God. They know they are not that God. They know they desperately need that God. They will frequently be found on their knees. If they are married, they will want prayer at the center of the marriage. If they are parents, they will pray daily with their children. If they meet with others to help them grow spiritually, they will make prayer a central part of those times, and not a small addendum. If they are leaders, they will call their people to prayer. They will pray with others and not just plan. They will put more confidence in prayer than in their own insight, skill, experience and instincts. Major repentance is needed in these areas in many of our lives, but we must understand that our failure shows not just a lack of discipline or lack of will, but a lack of humility. We are often confident that we can get the job done on our own. We might not say this, but our actions speak loudly.

After many years of successful church planting, Paul would still write:

> Not that we are competent in ourselves to claim anything for ourselves, but our competence comes from God. He has made us competent as ministers of a new covenant—not of the letter but of the Spirit; for the letter kills, but the Spirit gives life. (2 Corinthians 3:5-6)

Paul knew he was in the kingdom because of God. He knew he had succeeded in the kingdom because of God. He was a multi-talented man, but his confidence was not in his talent. He knew that only God could make his ministry flourish. Listen in on his correspondence with fellow disciples of Jesus to whom he was a father in the faith:

> He has delivered us from such a deadly peril, and he will deliver us. On him we have set our hope that he will continue to deliver us, as you help us by your prayers. Then many will give thanks on our behalf for the gracious favor granted us in answer to the prayers of many. (2 Corinthians 1:10-11)
>
> ...for I know that through your prayers and the help given by the Spirit of Jesus Christ, what has happened to me will turn out for my deliverance. (Philippians 1:19)
>
> And pray for us, too, that God may open a door for our message, so that we may proclaim the mystery of Christ, for which I am in chains. (Colossians 4:3)
>
> Brothers, pray for us. (1 Thessalonians 5:25)
>
> Finally, brothers, pray for us that the message of the Lord may spread rapidly and be honored, just as it was with you. (2 Thessalonians 3:1)

Here we see a humble leader—one fully convinced that he needed others to be praying for him. We will look at humility and leadership more later, but, leaders, here is a vital question for you: Do you frequently, sincerely and with deep conviction ask others to pray for your work? Do you feel you need to do that? Are you convinced that you will not succeed without it?

However, as you think about asking others to pray for you, don't just go get your organizer and add this to your to-do list. Deep change needs to come at a heart level. Are you seeing your own lack of competence? Are you understanding that God is the one who makes things grow? Do you resist looking needy to your fellow Christians? I know leaders who hate that word "needy," but that is what we are!

Humility is intimately related to prayer. Humility drives us to pray. Humility compels us to ask others to pray for us. Humility is what will cause our prayers to be heard.

▪ Thought Question ▪

Is there sufficient evidence in your prayer life to convict you, if you were on trial for showing humility?

NOTES
*Andrew Murray, *Humility* (Springdale, Penn.: Whitaker House, reprint 1982), 68.

chapter 6

walk humbly with your God

Part 2: Obedience and Surrender

Humility will have a profound impact on our spirituality. It will affect the quality of our faith and the depth of our prayers. In this chapter we will see that humility will also lead us to obey God and to surrender to his purposes, plans and providence. The man or woman who walks humbly with God will sing many songs, but "I Did It My Way" will not be one of them.

Humility and Obedience

There is an old story about the farm boy who went off to agricultural college and came back home to his "Pa" with all his newfound knowledge. The father asked the son to go to the north field and plant corn. The son tested the soil, found that corn would definitely grow there and so planted corn. The father asked the son to plant oats in the east field. The son tested the soil and found it compatible with oats and so planted oats. The father asked the son to go to the west field and plant wheat. The son, again, tested the soil, found that wheat would prosper and so planted wheat. Finally, the father asked the son to go to the south field and plant barley. The son tested the soil, concluded that it was unhealthy for barley, and so he planted rye. How obedient was the son? The answer is not seventy-five percent obedient, but totally disobedient. He only did what his father wanted when he agreed with the decision. He, with his college education, thought he knew better. Too often our obedience to God is dependent upon our agreement with God. This is not obedience.

Humility and obedience are definitely two sides of the same coin in Scripture, just as the opposites, arrogance and disobedience, are two sides of the wrong coin. A clear example of arrogance and disobedience is found in Israel's first king, Saul.

In 1 Samuel 15:1 we read that Samuel the prophet says to Saul, "I am the one the LORD sent to anoint you king over his people Israel; so *listen* now to the message from the LORD" (emphasis added). The message then given was clear. The Amalekites were to be punished by God for their treatment of the Hebrews coming out of Egypt. The judgment was intense. Saul was to "totally destroy everything that belongs to them" (v3). "Everything" meant everything! Saul proceeded to obey until verse 9: "But Saul and the army spared Agag and the best of the sheep and cattle, the fat calves and lambs—everything that was good." (He obviously defined "everything" differently. Maybe he had been to agricultural college!) "These they were unwilling to destroy completely, but everything that was despised and weak they totally destroyed."

God was then grieved that he had made Saul king because of Saul's failure to carry out *God's* instructions (v11). In his arrogance Saul had convinced himself that he had done basically what God wanted. He proudly proclaimed to the prophet Samuel when he reached him after the event: 'The LORD bless you! I have carried out the LORD's instructions." Samuel's sad, almost humorous, response cuts through to the reality: "What then is this bleating of sheep in my ears? What is this lowing of cattle that I hear?" (v14). What follows is God's revelation concerning what he truly values and some great insights for those wanting to learn humility:

> But Samuel replied:
>
> "Does the LORD delight in burnt offerings and sacrifices
>   as much as in *obeying the voice* of the LORD?
> To *obey* is better than sacrifice,
>   and to heed is better than the fat of rams.
> For rebellion is like the sin of divination,
>   and arrogance like the evil of idolatry.

> Because you have *rejected the word* of the Lord,
> he has rejected you as king."
> (1 Samuel 15:22-23, emphasis added)

First, we see in this text that arrogance and pride are the same sins as rebellion and idolatry. Hebrew parallelism was a literary device used for emphasis: A verse would be repeated in a slightly different form to doubly and emphatically make the point. In other words, if you missed it the first time, then maybe the second verse, stated slightly differently, would get to you. Verse 23 is an example of parallelism: *Rebellion* is like *divination; arrogance* is like *idolatry.*

It is easy to see the similarity between divination and idolatry. But do we see the similarity between rebellion and arrogance? Do we see the seriousness of the sins of rebellion, divination and idolatry, and miss the deadly seriousness of arrogance? It is difficult for us, in our pride, to grasp that the worship of idols and the practice of witchcraft are in the same category with arrogance. Yet, to God, all these words are synonyms of the same sin and attitude and describe someone who has placed himself at the center of life, who does not submit to God.

Second, arrogance is self-deceiving. Saul is totally oblivious to his sin. The very nature of arrogance makes one confident that he is right, even if others disagree. He thinks, *Who are they, and what do they know anyway?* Saul has convinced himself of his rightness. He is a leader out of control who proceeds to do things without precedent and without remorse. And yet so confident is he of his righteousness that Samuel actually finds him in Carmel where he had gone to "set up a monument in his own honor" (v12). What kind of monument? Was it a statue of himself? Is it really that hard to see the relationship of arrogance to idolatry? It is not hard for others to see—just hard for us to see it in ourselves!

The only hope we have of overcoming pride and self-deception is to welcome others into our lives. So many times when others point out to me what they see, I am dumbfounded. I do not see it at all, because without knowing it, I have slipped into a pride that is self-deceived. It is essential to have the right attitude toward the input of others. Saul received input, but his defensiveness kept him from repentance. He shifted the blame, justified himself and did everything we should not do when those around us love us enough to tell us the truth.

Third, humility means obedience in *everything*. Verse one places the emphasis on listening to God. Verse 22 reemphasizes the essentiality of "obeying the voice of the Lord." Saul practiced a selective obedience. He basically followed what God asked. He was mostly obedient. Surely he was close enough to compliance. The shock to most people is that God indeed expects exact and complete obedience. Anything else on our part is prideful: We are reasoning that we know better.

Sometimes when people from a religious background study the Bible more seriously, they come to the point where they are aware that they have not actually been following God's word. Their response tends to go in one of two directions: Some see their lack of compliance to God's standards and direction. They humbly submit to whatever God wants them to do, whether it is to repent of some sin or even to examine their initial commitment to God to see if it was truly sincere and correct in attitude and form. Others, however, proudly, and even literally, stiffen up. You can see the defensiveness, and even the rationalizations, when they exclaim, "Surely, just because I haven't done it exactly like the Bible says, I'm not condemned. What God really cares about anyway is what is going on in the heart." What God really cares about is, in fact, having *an obedient heart!* It does not matter what sacrifices and offerings you have made or even all the great things you have done for the Lord. What he wants is a humble and obedient spirit in his followers.

But exact obedience is not just for those initially studying the Bible. It is required *especially of leaders*. King Saul is the example to us that no matter what role we may have—elder, evangelist, teacher, ministry leader—no one is at liberty to play fast and loose with the commands of God. Saul was one of a kind, yet God removed from him his right to lead because of his lack of humility and obedience. His sins may not have seemed as serious as some that would be committed by David, but David found forgiveness because of his broken and contrite heart and genuine eagerness to repent. Saul was removed because of his arrogance.

As a leader, I have found myself at times beginning to think that I was above little details of obedience. I was mainly honest about the statistical data concerning the church. I did not need to personally be an example in my evangelism since it was my job just to equip everyone else. My prayer life did not need to be exemplary as long as I planned well. My slight exaggerations with examples were not that important as long as I was inspirational. In other words, I knew what God really was after, and if I slipped up here and there, that was still fine. Such thoughts now make me shiver! *Who do I think I am?* Are leaders above the law? Absolutely not! In fact they are judged even more strictly. How does God feel?

> "I am grieved that I have made Saul king, because he has turned away from me and *has not carried out my instructions.*" (1 Samuel 15:11, emphasis added)

If we are truly humble, we obey. We obey everything God has commanded, even in matters of detail. If we arrogantly think we know what God really means and think we are above literal compliance, then we are disciples of King Saul, not of Jesus Christ, who said of his relationship with God that:

> "The world must learn that I love the Father and that I do *exactly* what my Father has *commanded* me." (John 14:31, emphasis added)

Humility and Surrender

At a leadership conference in Israel I was on my first tour of Biblical sites. At Bethlehem we visited the traditional site of

Jesus' birth. To enter the large church edifice built over this place, one had to enter a small, low gate—known as the "humility gate"—the premise being, if you were too proud to bend, you were not welcome to visit the humble place of Jesus' birth, the manger in a stable. I have little information about the physical descriptions of the pearly gates of heaven, but I am sure that the proud have trouble entering there as well. Make no mistake about it: Heaven is for the humble. As David said:

> Though the LORD is on high, he looks upon the lowly,
>   but the proud he knows from afar. (Psalm 138:6)
>
> You save the humble
>   but bring low those whose eyes are haughty.
>   (Psalm 18:27)

Throughout Biblical history man has engaged in an ongoing struggle with God. The history of man's rebellion begins in the garden, continuing on throughout the Old Testament into the New. In a parable of Jesus, the tenants of a vineyard see the owner send his son to work things out with them. But Jesus describes their response:

> "But when the tenants saw the son, they said to each other, 'This is the heir. Come, let's kill him and take his inheritance.' So they took him and threw him out of the vineyard and killed him." (Matthew 21:38-39)

The tenants, of course, represent mankind, and the owner is God. Man, in his arrogance and pride, believes he can refuse to surrender to God's rule, his kingdom and his lordship.

For centuries God has been trying to get his people to see a simple message: *Surrender and live; resist and die.* Listen to the words of Jeremiah:

> "Furthermore, tell the people, 'This is what the LORD says: See, I am setting before you *the way of life and the way of death.* Whoever stays in this city will die by the sword,

famine or plague. But whoever goes out and surrenders to the Babylonians who are besieging you will live; he will escape with his life.'" (Jeremiah 21:8-9, emphasis added)

Follow the details closely: Jerusalem is surrounded by God's agent of judgment, the Babylonians. Due to internal revolt back in Babylon, King Zedekiah took hope that Nebuchadnezzar's state of distraction would allow Judea the opportunity for revolt. The Judean king sends a delegation to inquire from the prophet Jeremiah with the hope, "Perhaps the LORD will perform wonders for us as in times past so that he will withdraw from us" (Jeremiah 21:2b). There is an air of spirituality. Zedekiah even frees the slaves according to the requirements of the Law (see chapter 34). There is the hope of success as the Babylonians are distracted and withdraw to deal with an approaching Egyptian army. In their apparent deliverance, King Zedekiah, with the pressure off, reneges on his commitment and cancels his emancipation of the slaves.

Jeremiah gives a straightforward prophecy. The weapons of war and their stronghold of Jerusalem are doomed:

> "This is what the LORD, the God of Israel, says: I am about to turn against you the weapons of war that are in your hands, which you are using to fight the king of Babylon and the Babylonians who are outside the wall besieging you." (Jeremiah 21:4a)

Their only hope is to surrender, to no longer fight against God (in whatever form that takes) and accept God's discipline and control over their lives. They must confess their humanity and let God be God.

If you are considering becoming a Christian, or if you are already a Christian and are struggling with submitting to God's will, the choice is the same: Surrender and live; fight on and lose it all. King Zedekiah did not submit to God's word as it came through Jeremiah. The Babylonians breached the walls; Zedekiah fled during the night. He and his sons were captured.

On the orders of Nebuchadnezzar, he was forced to witness his sons' execution, and then his eyes were put out. His last sight was a reminder of the truth that he had resisted! The humble man is confident that God's way is better, and he surrenders his will to God's. The prideful one fears surrender and fights it but always loses in the end.

Surrender is the state we stay in as disciples of Christ, who himself constantly acknowledged his surrender to God. In the Garden of Gethsemane Jesus was strongly pulled in a certain direction, but in humility, he surrendered to the will of God. That surrender brought salvation for all who put their faith in him.

In the good times and the bad times, we need to be reminded of our complete dependence upon God and his complete sovereignty over our lives. Resistance has its root in only one place: our pride, our notion that we can better run things. We have our fine-sounding arguments which we rehearse in our minds, convincing ourselves of the justice of our cause. These are the strongholds that humility in relationships helps demolish as we help each other to take captive every thought and make it obedient to Christ (2 Corinthians 10:4-5). But the root is still pride! Surrender is that wonderful state of putting our lives into God's hands and trusting. Nothing brings greater peace!

• Thought Question •

What recent actions in your life demonstrate obedience and surrender?

chapter 7

what humility is not

A recent article in the *Washington Post* with the headline "Panel Examines Failings of Religious Leadership" began with this statement: "Pride, weak faith, ...and a lack of personal responsibility are among the failings of today's religious leaders in all denominations."* How could so-called religious leaders get it so wrong about such basic Christian practice? Why is humility not expected? Why do some of us who do want to seriously follow Jesus not pursue humility with more passion? The answer, in part, may be that there are real misunderstandings about what humility is all about. As much as we need to understand what humility is, we also need to understand what it is not.

First, authentic humility is not passiveness. In the minds of many people, "meekness" and "humility" are words describing those timid souls who never step up and take action. But the Bible uses these words to describe Moses, Jesus and Paul—not exactly Casper-Milquetoast-type guys.

God obviously wants his people to make a great impact on the world. He also expects them to be humble. The simple conclusion is that humble men and women will have great impact. They will not be people who sit on the sidelines letting everyone else influence and determine the direction of events. They will understand that on their own they cannot act wisely, but they will believe that with God they can act in powerful and decisive ways.

Second, humility is not cowardice in pious clothing. In actual fact, humility and courage always go together. The man who humbles himself under God's mighty hand will be ready to act with courage when others melt away. A careful look at Acts 4 shows us this combination of qualities in the early Christians. First, we hear the observation of the leaders of the Sanhedrin, the Jewish ruling council:

> When they saw the courage of Peter and John and realized that they were unschooled, ordinary men, they were astonished and they took note that these men had been with Jesus. (Acts 4:13)

The Jewish leaders are here describing men who were filled with the Holy Spirit, men trained by Jesus, and men who had by now understood Jesus' message about humility (Matthew 18:1-4). Even more than what these Jewish leaders understood, "these men had been with Jesus." These disciples of Jesus had changed. They had become like little children, and they had entered the kingdom. But what do others notice about them? Their courage. We must get this straight: Humble men and women are not shrinking violets. They are not found cowering in a corner someplace. Because they are in awe of God, they are no longer afraid of men. Listen to what happens next:

> Then they called them in again and commanded them not to speak or teach at all in the name of Jesus. But Peter and John replied, "Judge for yourselves whether it is right in God's sight to obey you rather than God. For we cannot help speaking about what we have seen and heard." (Acts 4:18-20)

This was not some arrogant reply from rebellious men. It was a firm, courageous stand taken by men of faith, conviction and humility. You see this clearly when you examine what happens next:

> After further threats they let them go. They could not decide how to punish them, because all the people were

> praising God for what had happened. For the man who was miraculously healed was over forty years old.
> On their release, Peter and John went back to their own people and reported all that the chief priests and elders had said to them. When they heard this, they raised their voices together in prayer to God....
> After they prayed, the place where they were meeting was shaken. And they were all filled with the Holy Spirit and spoke the word of God boldly. (Acts 4:21-24, 31)

Upon their release, Peter and John do not boast about their courage, nor do they try to handle things on their own. They first go back to their people (expressing their need for the fellowship), and then they lead the people to go to God (expressing their need for him). And where does such humility end up? With men and women out speaking the word of God boldly. Humility is not timidity or cowardice!

Let us consider an especially sensitive area in which confusion often reigns. We are thinking here about how to treat relatives who oppose us because of our faith. What is the right thing? Do we say nothing and passively take verbal abuse? Do we argue? Do we let unfair, critical comments about the church go uncontested? Do we think, "I'll defend Jesus but not my fellow Christians in the church"? How do we get our families to respect our beliefs and even to be influenced by our faith in Christ? Do we impact them by being passive or by sharing our convictions with sincerity and love? The answers need to come from the Scriptures, and there are few passages better than 2 Timothy 2:24-26:

> And the Lord's servant must not quarrel; instead, he must be kind to everyone, able to teach, not resentful. Those who oppose him he must gently instruct, in the hope that God will grant them repentance leading them to a knowledge of the truth, and that they will come to their senses and escape from the trap of the devil, who has taken them captive to do his will.

Being kind to someone always means being considerate. Being considerate of them means respecting them. Respecting them means being willing to listen to them. This may be shocking to some, but our non-Christian relatives sometimes see things in us that we need to hear. Humility before them means that we are willing to listen. At the same time, it does not mean we do not speak. It just means we speak gently, and we do it without self-righteousness. It means we do it humbly, praying to God for their hearts to change, not trying to force them to change. Humility in such situations will always mean getting godly advice from others as you learn to affect those relationships that mean so much. But remember: Humility does not mean that you do not speak up.

Third, humility does not mean becoming a doormat. While the humble person will be willing to give up his rights for a greater good, humility does not inherently mean you let others abuse you. There are several occasions in the life of the apostle Paul in which his response almost catches us off guard. There are times when he does not hold on to his rights (1 Corinthians 9:15-18), but there are times when he forcefully declares them. One such incident follows his beating and imprisonment in Philippi for exorcising a demon from a fortune-telling girl. First, there was an earthquake, and then came the amazing conversion of the Philippian jailer and his family. The next day, when the authorities were ready to dismiss the whole incident and send them on their way, Paul's response was quite assertive:

> The jailer told Paul, "The magistrates have ordered that you and Silas be released. Now you can leave. Go in peace."
> But Paul said to the officers [not the jailer who is now a brother]: "They beat us publicly without a trial, even though we are Roman citizens, and threw us into prison. And now do they want to get rid of us quietly? No! Let them come themselves and escort us out." (Acts 16:36-37)

We do not know all the reasons why Paul responded so forcefully. Perhaps it was to protect the newly founded church at

Philippi from governmental persecution. But for certain, Paul was not passive.

In a similar incident in Acts 23 Paul was struck for speaking and responded quite forcibly in his defense. Being humble does not mean saying nothing nor failing to take advantage of one's rights. Cross bearing always means that we are willing to let go of our rights, but it does not always mean silently taking abuse. In Jesus' life there were times when he was silent and times when he spoke forcefully. Humility means wanting to do the righteous thing in those circumstances, not just the thing that comes out of self.

Fourth, genuine humility is not just "lip service." It is not just outward form. Listen to these words from Jesus:

> He [Jesus] replied, "Isaiah was right when he prophesied about you hypocrites; as it is written:
> "'These people honor me with their lips,
>   but their hearts are far from me.'" (Mark 7:6)
>
> "What do you think? There was a man who had two sons. He went to the first and said, 'Son, go and work today in the vineyard.'
> "'I will not,' he answered, but later he changed his mind and went.
> "Then the father went to the other son and said the same thing. He answered, 'I will, sir,' but he did not go.
> "Which of the two did what his father wanted?"
> "The first," they answered. (Matthew 21:28-31)

Humility is not walking around saying all the right words, seeming to be compliant and willing, but inside having another agenda. Humility is not walking around playing the religious game, as in Jesus' day, dressed religiously, talking religiously with quiet, calm, soft-spoken tones, having a veneer of religiosity, but inside being full of pride. Even in the Old Testament, we hear this challenge, as God's people begin playing the religious game:

> "As for you, son of man, your countrymen are talking together about you by the walls and at the doors of the houses, saying to each other, 'Come and hear the message that has come from the LORD.' My people come to you, as they usually do, and sit before you to listen to your words, but they do not put them into practice. With their mouths they express devotion, but their hearts are greedy for unjust gain. Indeed, to them you are nothing more than one who sings love songs with a beautiful voice and plays an instrument well, for they hear your words but do not put them into practice." (Ezekiel 33:30-32)

The inside must match the outside, or the outside is nothing at all.

Finally, humility is not blindly following. In Galatians 2 Paul found himself in a situation in which one of the "pillars" of the church, Peter, was behaving in a compromising fashion. Due to a fear of some of the brothers from Jerusalem who might look with disdain upon eating with the Gentile Christians, Peter withdrew from the Gentiles, causing tension and disunity in the Antioch church. Paul responded:

> When I saw that they were not acting in line with the truth of the gospel, I said to Peter in front of them all, "You are a Jew, yet you live like a Gentile and not like a Jew. How is it, then, that you force Gentiles to follow Jewish customs?" (Galatians 2:14)

It did not matter that Peter was "the rock," the leader of the Twelve. Paul had to speak the truth in this situation if the gospel message was being threatened. Was Paul proud? I think not, but being humble had nothing to do with being quiet while something wrong was happening. Being a conflict avoider is not to be equated with being a humble disciple of Jesus. And if leaders as strong and spiritual as Peter can leave the "straight and narrow," then everyone in the church needs fellow Christians to speak the truth humbly to them at times.

Whether we are dealing with others in the church or with others, we must always obey God rather than men. Disciples of

Jesus must learn to highly value submission. We must have deep convictions that submission is from God. We must totally disagree when we hear that the president of the National Organization of Women declares that "submission to another human being is always wrong." However, we must never forget that ultimately we are to submit to God, and that submission to men must always fit within God's will—or else we cannot obey. Humility never means blindly following. It never means, "Yes, sir, I will do that just because you say so." We must respond only to God in that way. Blind obedience is not humility; it is foolishness.

Humility often has a bad name. A closer look shows us that this is undeserved. True humility is not passiveness, it is not cowardice, it does not become a doormat, it is not a pious act and it is not foolishness. True humility is full of wisdom; it takes heart and faith; it is heroic and bears good fruit.

• Thought Question •
How have false ideas affected your attitude toward humility?

NOTES

*"Panel Examines Failings of Religious Leadership," *Washington Post*, March 11, 1998.

chapter 8

God's work in humbling us

A few weeks before I wrote this chapter, a few of my friends from Ohio and I went fishing on Lake Erie at the beginning of the season for walleye, the celebrated game fish of that area. These were all men I oversee in the ministry, and I was excited to spend time with them and to show off my self-professed prowess as a fisherman. As the leader, one likes to lead in everything. The experience was full of excitement, expectation and the thrill of the hunt, as we cast our lines out. What I was not expecting was that the least experienced fisherman would catch the biggest fish (a Fish-Ohio-Award size!) and that I would catch absolutely nothing. What was going on? What had I done wrong? Why was this happening to me now? Was God trying to humble me? Does God even care if I catch any fish? Does he even care about my embarrassment and shame?

I don't know whether God is concerned about the number of fish I catch or not, though there were several times in the Gospels he certainly did have an impact on such endeavors. But the Scriptures are clear that God is very concerned with the kind of man I am meant to be and the kind of heart I am meant to have. He will actively oppose me if I am proud. Where or how he opposes me is all theoretical, but oppose me he will. Whenever we find that something seems to be holding back our efforts, it is always good to ask, "Might God be opposing me here because of my pride?"

From Paul's autobiographical section in 2 Corinthians 12 we see clearly that spiritually minded people can be tempted with pride, *and* that God gets involved to keep them humble. Paul describes great revelations he received, but then he says, "To keep me from becoming conceited...there was given me a thorn in my flesh" (2 Corinthians 12:7). The message is plain: Having seen things that other men had not seen, Paul could very easily have become proud in his unique knowledge. To keep that from happening, God allowed something most unpleasant in Paul's life, something Paul neither wanted nor understood at the time. Later on, however, after his prayers for relief went unanswered, it became clear to him that God was working all along to keep him humble. Our God is not passive. He is actively working for our humility. But are we getting the point?

Joseph: A Case Study

If we make a few reasonable assumptions, Joseph's story in Genesis may give us a good look at the whole process of God's "humbling" and "lifting up" in a man's life. The story begins in chapter 37.

Scene One

> Joseph, a young man of seventeen, was tending the flocks with his brothers, the sons of Bilhah and the sons of Zilpah, his father's wives, and he brought their father a bad report about them. (Genesis 37:2)

Here the young man, the son of the favorite wife, tattles on the sons of the slave women (not the proper wives), his older half-brothers. Is there not an unspoken air of pride in this text?

Scene Two

> Now Israel loved Joseph more than any of his other sons, because he had been born to him in his old age; and he made a richly ornamented robe for him. When his brothers saw that their father loved him more than any of them, they hated him and could not speak a kind word to him. (Genesis 37:3-4)

Nothing is said specifically about Joseph's attitude or arrogance, but when a young man is given special attention and feels the animosity of his siblings, it is quite normal for there to be pride and even smugness on his part. Was he oblivious to and unfazed by all this special attention? I think not.

Scene Three
Joseph had a dream, and when he told it to his brothers, they hated him all the more. (Genesis 37:5)

The dream was not that complex in its basic meaning. Joseph related it clearly, "We were all binding sheaves in the field when mine rose up and yours all bowed down to mine." I'm sure that they did not exclaim to their brother, "Thanks for sharing that with us!" Did the future-celebrated dream interpreter not figure this one out?

Scene Four
Then he had another dream, and he told it to his brothers. "Listen," he said, "I had another dream, and this time the sun and moon and eleven stars were bowing down to me." (Genesis 37:9)

Even his not-so-astute brothers could not miss the point. He was exalting himself. His brothers hated him even more, and his father, Jacob, rebuked him.

Here is the picture: Joseph, the young man of seventeen, favored in his father's love, corrected his brothers and predicted their subservience to him, with even his parents paying him homage. What teenager could have handled this without some degree of cockiness or arrogance? God had a grand plan to use Joseph in a mighty way to save many. However, he needed God's hand in his life to change his character and make him into a humble man that God could use.

In his ensuing life struggles, there is abundant evidence that God's hand was on him, God's hand that humbles and his hand that lifts up. The young dreamer was sold by his brothers and became a slave to Potiphar in Egypt. He was falsely accused of attempted rape by Potiphar's wife and ended up in prison. Can you imagine the conditions of a prison in ancient Egypt? But there he was introduced to prominent men in the Egyptian hierarchy, particularly the cupbearer, who would one day recall Joseph's assistance and dream interpreting ability at just the right time.

Through it all God was humbling the young man in unjust situations, yet training Joseph to trust him. By the time Joseph became the trusted aide to Pharaoh, he could see how God had been working in it all. It is my conviction that God used Joseph in amazing ways, but only after God had changed him into a different man.

An Attitude to Imitate

But what enabled Joseph to learn what God was teaching? As Jacob prepared for his death, he gathered his sons around to give them a prophetic blessing. Going through his sons one by one, he finally came to Joseph and, not surprisingly, gave him the longest blessing. He described the qualities that were in Joseph's life that enabled him to learn from God's humbling hand. His father's comments give us three important insights. Our conclusion will be that Joseph made three decisions that determined his attitude—decisions that all Christians need to make if they are to be shaped into the kind of men and women God can use.

First, Joseph decided to be a man constantly dependent on God. "Joseph is a fruitful vine, a fruitful vine near a spring," said his father (Genesis 49:22). I have a strong suspicion that the meaning here is related to the fact that a spring is not a river. A spring, unlike most of the rivers of Palestine, flows all the time. In arid lands one often finds riverbeds that periodically are filled with water. But during the droughts, all that is left is an empty channel. The level of vegetation growth in such a place is up and down, depending on the climatic conditions. By contrast, a vine growing by a spring has a continual source of support and refreshment. Joseph was not dependent on changing outward circumstances, but on a faithful and trustworthy God. He was planted by a spring, not by an unpredictable river! In Potiphar's house he relied on God; in prison he relied on God; before Pharaoh he relied on God. God placed him in circumstances that forced and taught him to rely on God, not man.

Too many times our spiritual growth is dependent on our outward circumstances. "I'm having a good year, and everything is working out"; or "I'm having a hard time; my situation is not that good." Too many times in my life I have been just that way. But God allowed those hard times in order to humble me and to teach me dependence. Sadly, I have often resisted with moodiness and discontentment. When that happens, valuable lessons are missed, and we see real weaknesses in our walk with God.

Second, Joseph decided to believe in God's providence. Joseph reassured his brothers, who were gripped by fear of retribution, by calling attention to God's bigger picture: "You intended to harm me, but God intended it for good to accomplish what is now being done, the saving of many lives" (Genesis 50:20). Again Jacob described his son as "a fruitful vine near a spring, whose branches climb over a wall" (Genesis 49:22). Walls are interesting obstacles. Our prideful natures can be tempted to smash through them! Joseph learned to grow *over* them! Those obstacles which could have stopped him became a support for his life as he rose above them.

Bitterness is a defiling sin that results when we refuse to accept God's humbling work in our lives. We hit the walls, and instead of growing over them and making them a support for serious spiritual growth, resentment and bitterness take over. Those walls become monuments and symbols in our lives of our unhappiness. As with the Great Wall of China, we can see our walls from space: No matter how far we get from them, they are ever before us as reminders of our pain or our frustration. Joseph is amazing because, despite serious abuses by his brothers, injustice from Potiphar and the forgetfulness of the cupbearer, he grew more humble, not bitter.

Joseph's learned humility is demonstrated by the number of references to his expressions of heartfelt affection. Joseph wept in Genesis 43:30, 45:2, 45:14-15, 46:29, 50:1 and 50:17. He cried all the time! Far from being hardened and embittered, his heart was tender and soft. Even the thought that his brothers were fearful of him and the idea of seeking vengeance brought him to tears. In contrast, his brothers were embittered by their father's favoritism of Joseph and haunted by the guilt of what they had done.

> They said to one another, "Surely we are being punished because of our brother. We saw how distressed he was when he pleaded with us for his life, but we would not listen; that's why this distress has come upon us." (Genesis 42:21)

No tears are ever mentioned on their part, and their hardness and bitterness demonstrated itself in ongoing fear, doubt and suspicion. This is the outcome for those who are faithless and have no humble confidence in God's providence.

My greatest struggles as a disciple of Jesus have come as I have resented and resisted God's use of circumstances and men in my life to teach me humility. I have always done what I had to do, thank God, but regrettably, sometimes with an attitude that I was being forced to do it. Moving from Australia, where I had served for thirteen years, to Washington, D.C., was more difficult for me than anything had been up until that point. I exerted so much effort—all wasted—by blaming others, unhappily following orders and being reluctant to give my heart to new people. I came to my wall and sat on it. And I paid the price. Joseph in contrast climbed over every wall by faith and trusted that God was in control. To his brothers' amazement, he explained to them at the moment of disclosure:

> "And now, do not be distressed and do not be angry with yourselves for selling me here, because it was to save lives that *God sent me* ahead of you.... So then, it was not *you* who sent me here, but God." (Genesis 45:5, 8, emphasis added)

Third, Joseph made the decision to be confident about the blessings that come from the Almighty. Again, in Jacob's words:

> With *bitterness* archers attacked him;
>   they shot at him with hostility.
> But his bow remained steady,
>   his strong arms stayed *limber*,
> because of the hand of the Mighty One of Jacob,
>   because of the Shepherd, the Rock of Israel,
> because of your father's God, who helps you,
>   because of the Almighty, who blesses you
> with blessings of the heavens above,
>   blessings of the deep that lies below,
>   blessings of the breast and womb.
>   (Genesis 49:23-25, emphasis added)

Jacob honored his son for recognizing his need for God and allowing God to help him. Joseph apparently allowed the experiences of his life to teach him that, while life does not usually work out the way we thought it would, God never stops blessing us. Joseph was humbled by life, but that led him to look to the Almighty and not to himself for blessings.

God loves us so much and wants to bless us so much that he allows events and people to interact with our lives in ways that we would never consciously choose. God's active process of humbling us is not to make our lives miserable but to truly make our lives awesome. What is essential is reminding ourselves of his power and goodness even when bitter arrows fly our way. All this allowed Joseph to stay limber—not only physically but spiritually. There is a spiritual limberness needed when we are under fire—when the arrows are flying—that allows God to shape us into the kind of vessels that can be used gloriously for his church. We must be able to roll with the punches, confident that God's blessings will always come.

God does humble us, like it or not. God uses the painful and the difficult experiences to train us. Some of us may be humbled through financial failures, some through family and marriage problems. Others of us may know physical or emotional struggles that show our weakness. Some will be fired from jobs and some asked to step out of spiritual leadership roles. Whether his humbling does any good depends on our attitude. We need: first, to be planted by the spring (our ongoing relationship with God); second, a conviction that our God truly reigns and directs our lives; and last, complete confidence in the blessings that will come from God!

• Thought Question •
What circumstances has God used to humble you and how did you respond?

part two

**humility
and
relationships**

chapter 9

humility toward all people

We may acknowledge the greatness of God. We may fall in humility before him in prayer, but the real test of our humility is what we do when we leave that place and go out and meet our neighbors. Andrew Murray is surely right when he says that humility toward men will be the only proof that our humility before God is real.

Paul told Titus how to train the church to have great relationships in a world in which relationships are such a mess:

> Remind the people to be subject to rulers and authorities, to be obedient, to be ready to do whatever is good, to slander no one, to be peaceable and considerate, and to show true humility toward all men. (Titus 3:1-2)

Humility is to be shown to *all* men—not just to fellow Christians, not just to people who think the way we do, not just to people who are kind and treat us well, but to *all* men—to the good, the bad and the ugly.

All of our relationships, from those with family members, to those with fellow believers, to those with people who oppose us, are to be conducted in humility. Humility in all relationships is God's will and God's command. Humility toward God comes to an abrupt end if we are prideful in our dealings with others.

Earlier we examined some misconceptions about humility, but now we must explore more fully what it does mean to be *completely* humble (Ephesians 4:2) in the everyday affairs of our lives. We must learn what Peter means when he says: "Clothe yourselves with humility toward one another" (1 Peter 5:5).

Andrew Murray is correct when he says, "The 'insignificances' of daily life are the 'importances' and tests of eternity. It is in our most unguarded moments that we show who we really are."* We may do very well when we are able to prepare and follow a script. We may relate quite humbly as we meet with others at church or as we stand before the assembly. But the real test is, how do we respond to that unexpected phone call, that unanticipated problem, that uninvited visitor? How do we treat the man who just rear-ended us or the waitress who just brought us the wrong order? How do we respond when we find that the Christian we are helping has, for the fourth time, not followed through with the plans we had agreed to with him? What do we say and do in those unscripted moments?

> The good man brings good things out of the good stored up in his heart, and the evil man brings evil things out of the evil stored up in his heart. For out of the overflow of his heart his mouth speaks. (Luke 6:45)

What flows out of our mouths in those everyday affairs, those non-stained-glass moments? What does it reveal about what is deep inside us? Is humility an act with us? Is it clothing only to be worn on "holy days"? Or has our time before God affected us to the core? In all circumstances are we aware that we are, in the words of a great spiritual, "standing in his presence on Holy Ground"? Does our knowledge of the Holy affect the way we treat the paper boy, our coworkers, our children and our spouses?

In the following chapters we will look at how humility should be found in specific relationships. In this chapter we want to look at some general principles for showing "true humility toward all men."

Without Self-Righteousness

Few expressions of pride are more common than self-righteousness—and don't think for a minute that the problem is limited to the Pharisees or even to "religious" people. I have met few, if any, unbelievers who were not self-righteous. Most of them consider themselves better than the religious people they know, because, in their words, "At least I am not a hypocrite." Others feel superior to those who practice faith because they don't need the "crutch" of religion. Almost all people are adept at spotting flaws in others that they can use to build their case for being as good as or better than someone else.

But true humility means an end to all of our self-righteousness. If becoming a disciple of Jesus causes you to be more self-righteous, you have missed the message of the cross. Now, the actions of some non-Christians make it easy for us to be tempted with this expression of pride. As Christians, we are exposed to incredible depravity, immorality, amorality and arrogance in the world which, in turn, tempts us to feel superior. Around us we also see all kinds of counterfeit expressions of faith that tempt us to say, "Lord, I thank you that I am not like this man," or "...that our church is not like that one."

But if we are serious about humility, we must be serious about self-righteousness. We must see what a silly and foolish thing it is. I am convinced about this, and yet I am vulnerable to self-righteousness and must be honest about that. I know there are still many situations waiting for me that will bring my self-righteousness to the forefront. I must be ready to confess, repent and change when it is exposed in me.

When I recently traveled to Israel, I observed the members of the ultra-orthodox Jewish sect—the Haredi. There were dozens of them at the Wailing Wall. They now make up about fifteen percent of Israeli society. The men have the long beards and wear the traditional heavy, long, black coats and hats, even in the heat of summer (a carryover from their Eastern European roots).

One night at dinner in our Western-style hotel, I realized that one of the Haredi was observing *us*. He walked slowly through the hotel with his hands held behind his back, peering into the restaurants and sitting rooms, scowling at the sight of Americans and other foreigners. I learned before my trip that they considered us all—and their secular Jewish neighbors—to be desecrators of their land. He seemed to have no other business in the hotel save that of giving disapproving looks. He and I briefly passed each other as I walked from the restaurant. It was one of those unscripted moments. In the face of such a modern Pharisee, complete with all the outward signs of self-righteousness, my own heart was tested. It was hard to know how to respond to someone who probably regarded me as but a dog. Though we never exchanged words, I know for sure that my immediate heart reaction was not love and it was not humility.

Later I reflected on what I had felt. I was, at the very moment I saw this man, only a few blocks from where Jesus was placed on the cross, and yet, at that moment I did not think of the cross at all. I have always preached that the ground is level at the foot of the cross. I have always taught that when we stand at the foot of the cross, we cannot possibly look down on anyone, for we all are there as sinners for whom Christ died. And there I was, for the first time in my life, in the city where he was put to death. He died there for Tom, and he died there for Yitzhak Lebowitz (not his real name, just the only name of a Haredi that I know).

Yitzhak is a zealot, but then so am I. We express our passion for God in a very different way. I believe Yitzhak has what Paul's Jewish brothers had—a zeal for God that is not based on knowledge (Romans 10:2)—but there, without the grace of God, go I. And so I say, "Lord, increase my faith, increase my love, deepen my conviction about the cross. I am not better than this man." Yes, there for a moment in a Jerusalem hotel with the walls of the Old City clearly in sight, I felt I was better than he. I looked down on him, even as he looked down on me. But the cross has shown me how wrong that was. Thank God for Jesus. Yitzhak, please forgive me.

Self-righteousness is never justified. You can read the paper and hear all the horrible things human beings do to each other, and you can say, "Well at least I wouldn't do that," and maybe you wouldn't, but Jesus was harder on the self-righteous people than on all the murderers, adulterers and thieves combined. None of them had a whole chapter of a gospel written as an exposé of them. There must have been a reason for this. I don't think Jesus misread the situation. I don't think he just had a grudge against the ultra-religious. The self-righteous soul is a prideful soul.

Sometimes I hear us—no, sometimes I hear *myself*—scorning someone else's practice of religion. Sure, we need to be confronting error. We need to call things as they are, but I can get a self-righteous tone in my voice that is really saying, "We would not be so foolish as to do that or to think that is right before God." *God forgive me.*

We can see the falsity in others' lives. We can teach them clearly how they need to change, but we can do that without looking down on them, disparaging them and certainly without forgetting "there, but for the grace of God, go I."

We can also be self-righteous even in our own fellowship, even among people with whom we are like-minded. We can believe that our evangelism or our efforts in training others puts us above other people. God forbid, but we can even believe that our practice of prayer and humility makes us superior to others! As embarrassing as it is, I must plead guilty to that one—probably the worst one of all. It must not be tolerated.

When is the last time you asked a fellow Christian who knows you well if you ever appear to be self-righteous? How do you react to that possibility? That may very well be the only way some of us will see it. I have not done this in a long time, but before this book is released I will ask that question. The more I crucify self-righteousness, the more useful to God I will be.

With Forgiveness

We do not forgive others for two main reasons. Sometimes it is because we want the other person to hurt more for what they have done. We are not eager to give them any relief. We want them to pay more of an emotional price. At other times, it is because we feel we have a right to hold on to our hurt and nurse it a while longer. We are not ready to act cheerful and kind. We want to grieve over our pain. Forgiveness would mean closing the book, and we want to keep it open.

Humility means forgiving. See how Paul linked the two in his letter to the Colossians:

> Therefore, as God's chosen people, holy and dearly loved, clothe yourselves with compassion, kindness, humility, gentleness and patience. Bear with each other and forgive whatever grievances you may have against one another. Forgive as the Lord forgave you. (Colossians 3:12-13)

Humility and forgiveness are drawn from the same source. Our humility is rooted in the knowledge that our sins, though many, have all been forgiven and atoned for by the blood of Christ. Were it not for his sacrifice, we would still be in our sins, we would not have a relationship with God, and we would be on the road to destruction. But we have been redeemed and justified and sanctified, not because of our works—lest any man should boast—but because of God's mercy and grace (Ephesians 2:8-9). Any man or woman who walks away from such a scene and is not humble and forgiving toward his fellow Christian, his spouse or even his enemy is like that man who sees his face in the mirror and immediately forgets what he looks like. But God is not patient with such spiritual dementia.

In Matthew 18 Jesus told a poignant story to illustrate this point. There was a man who owed his master ten thousand talents. He was just a common servant. If he were living today in our economy, those ten thousand talents would equal something like ten million dollars. As a servant, he made a tiny salary, some saying that it would equal about seventeen cents a day in our money.

How did he get in such debt? Jesus is not concerned with that. It is a parable. He just wants us to realize that the man was in an absolutely hopeless situation. If he could put all of his salary on the debt each week (and had to use none of it to support his family), and if he paid no interest on the debt, it would still take him somewhere in the neighborhood of 183,000 years to pay off the debt! This makes what he says to the master either comical or pathetic: "Be patient with me and I will pay back all I owe." Sure.

The man then received the only thing that would help him: mercy. The master forgave the whole debt. But then the story turns ugly. The forgiven man leaves the site of massive forgiveness, goes and finds another man who owes him a hundred denari (about fifteen dollars in today's funds), and offers joyfully to forgive him. Sadly, that is not what it says. That is what should have happened, but Jesus says that he grabbed the man by the throat and said, "Pay me back all of what you owe." When his friend pleaded for mercy, the man who had been shown much, showed none and had his debtor thrown into prison.

But the forgiven man was a fool. The only logical and reasonable and moral thing would have been to treat others in the way that he had been treated. Because he did not do that, the master called him back in, revoked his mercy and had this arrogant fool thrown into prison. Jesus' terse ending is a forceful reminder to us that God expects us to be humble about the mercy we have received and to show mercy to others: "This is how my heavenly Father will treat each of you unless you forgive your brother from your heart" (Matthew 18:35).

Not forgiving is a supreme act of arrogance. Who do we think we are? This action says that the offenses committed against us are worse than those we have committed against God. Do we not see that we had the ten million dollar debt and that our friend had only the fifteen dollar debt? (I suspect Jesus is saying that *even the worst sin* committed against me is only the fifteen dollar debt compared to the millions I owe God.) We have been forgiven much and have been given much relief. Without mercy we would be doomed. There must not be in our lives a shocking ending to the story like we find in Matthew 18. Paul says to treat each other with humility, forgiving each other as God has forgiven us.

Being the Servant

To lead his spiritual movement Jesus chose twelve prideful souls, because it wasn't like there were other kinds from which to choose. He worked patiently for months to change them into humble disciples. But they were slow learners. At one point, well along in his work with them, pride erupted on all sides (Mark 10:35-45). James and John wanted the two places of preeminence in the kingdom. The other ten, equally competitive fellows, got wind of this request and were indignant. In the midst of this power struggle and crass demonstration of pride, Jesus taught his greatest lesson about being a servant:

> Jesus called them together and said, "You know that those who are regarded as rulers of the Gentiles lord it over them, and their high officials exercise authority over them. Not so with you. Instead, whoever wants to become great among you must be your servant, and whoever wants to be first must be slave of all." (Mark 10:42-44)

Instead of pride, he wanted to see humility. Instead of trying to push past each other to the front of the line, they needed to be serving each other. Pride wants to control people. Humility wants to serve them. Not everyone who serves is humble. But everyone who is humble will be a servant.

People do not serve others for several reasons. They may think that it makes them look bad. They may reason that they are too important and that serving is best done by those without such great demands on their schedules. They may see it as a misuse of talent. Certainly, it would be poor stewardship for a talented leader to spend all his time taking meals to others or cleaning the houses of his friends. But in every follower of Jesus there must be a clear understanding that goes like this: "I am not too good, too important, too talented or too anything to be a servant." Jesus' final comment in this section of Scripture makes that perfectly clear:

> "For even the Son of Man did not come to be served, but to serve, and to give his life as a ransom for many." (Mark 10:45)

Here is a very important question (and one you ought to ask of others who know you): Are you known as a servant? In the church? Among the leaders? On the job? In the neighborhood? Are you known as one who serves? Jesus was. And you want to be like him. Those of us living in modern Western culture may not be confronted by the abundance of needs that can be seen in the developing nations, but we still have ample opportunities to serve. People will always need help. Humility says, "I have been served, and now I want to serve others."

Most of us need advice about the best way we can serve and how to best use our talents, but all of us need hearts that say, "I am just an unworthy servant. I am only doing my duty" (Luke 17:10). And guess what? Those who serve discover there is joy and glory in serving. When you lose your life, you find it.

Looking down on no one. Forgiving everyone. Serving as Jesus served. This is showing humility toward all people.

• Thought Question •

What are your most honest thoughts about being humble toward everyone you know and those you will soon meet?

NOTES

*Murray, 44.

chapter 10

humility in 'discipling'

The words "disciple" and "disciples" appear more than two-hundred times in the New Testament. Jesus did not call men and women to become adherents to a religion. He called them to become his disciples. Discipling relationships, then, are relationships in which we are helping each other to be disciples of Jesus: relationships in which we encourage, correct, inspire and challenge each other to take all our gifts and abilities and fully use them to advance the mission of Jesus in this world. In discipling relationships people who are serious about following Jesus help each other to become more and more like Jesus Christ. Such relationships have no chance of working without humility. The very definition of a disciple implies and assumes humility.

On Discipling Others

As I worked on this chapter, our teen ministry leader came by wanting input. "Give me a challenge, tell me how I need to grow," he said. "Come on, just tell me, I can handle it! Teach me, I want to learn!" He hungers for advice and is keen on changing. As one of the people in his life helping him to grow spiritually, I want him to develop deep convictions about the word of God and to have an uncompromising commitment to the Scriptures. I want him to have boldness and zeal that will inspire others. I want to help him be focused, thorough and hard working. Most of all I want him to be able to come and learn humility from me, even as the disciples were invited to come learn humility from Jesus (Matthew 11:29). What are some key elements to remember as we try to impart humility in discipling relationships?

We need to remind ourselves whose disciples we all are. As Paul writes to the Romans (14:4) who were upset and bothered that some were not fitting in with the rest in opinion matters:

> Who are you to judge someone else's servant? To his own master he stands or falls. And he will stand, for the Lord is able to make him stand.

Paul is not saying that we should never give others direction for their spiritual lives. He clearly teaches that we should do just that a few verses later (Romans 15:14). But he does remind us to always remember that those we counsel are not *our* disciples, but God's. We are, at best, stewards working with God's people—not ours.

To the Corinthians who were quick to pick sides and claim ownership, Paul wrote: "For we are God's fellow workers; you are God's field, God's building" (1 Corinthians 3:9). Understanding God's ownership helps us to not take everything so personally. Yes, we need to be personally involved with those whom we are trying to help, but not emotionally possessive, taking every disappointment as if it were directed at us. If they are arrogant or unreliable, their sin is ultimately against God, not us. Peter charges elders to "be shepherds of God's flock...not lording it over those entrusted to you, but being examples to the flock" (1 Peter 5:2-3). With the use of the Greek word *katakurieontes,* translated "lording over," the implication is that the lordship is Christ's, not ours. We need to make sure we are not usurping that which belongs to him.

We must disciple from a position of openness. Nothing keeps us humble like being open. If we find ourselves expecting those we are helping to be open with us, but we would never dream of being open with them, we can be sure that our pride is deep rooted. Relationships need to be two-way streets. Discernment is necessary, but in principle there must be mutual openness. "Confess your sins one to another" (James 5:16) means just that.

We must show willingness to take input from those we lead. Throughout Scripture godly men listened to those younger and those they were leading. Job listened to the youngest of his friends, Elihu. David, who was the king, was convicted by Nathan. Naaman was brought to his senses and humbled by his servant girl. Apollos received the correction of a married couple far less influential than he was, and the veteran Peter was convicted by newcomer Paul's stance on doctrine and unity. Those who refused to listen to input, especially those kings of Israel, were the ones who paid the price in spiritual failure.

As an elder in the church and one often involved in various types of counseling, I have observed something that consistently shuts people down. For example, if the husband is fixated on his leadership to the point that he never gets input from his wife, if she is afraid to speak her mind, if he constantly shuts her down and effectively says, "Submit, never question me or challenge me," it is obvious that there will be marriage problems. In the same way, if a leader gets fixated on his leadership, if he never gets input from those who work with him, if he constantly shuts down all who attempt to influence him, what you have is tyranny and not discipling. Few people will become more like Jesus in such an environment.

If you have any hope of helping others to grow as disciples of Christ, you must be sure that they find you approachable and that they feel free to share anything with you, even something they see in your life that needs attention. If spiritual leaders do not have men and women around them willing to tell them the truth and if they do not welcome such truth, the very life of the church is endangered.

We must stay humble if we hope to be used by God to help disciple others. We must openly receive those who are spiritual, honest and brave enough to show us the specks (or even logs) in our eyes. Only then will we be able to see clearly enough to help others (Matthew 7:3-5). A prideful leader is a hypocrite in

God's kingdom. The solution is to be discipled yourself as you disciple others.

On Being Discipled

On the other side of the coin, we need to understand how vital humility is in receiving and applying discipling. At its very heart, being discipled—receiving input, teaching, correction and encouragement to become more like Jesus—is an exercise in humility. Being discipled means allowing other people to help us with our life and our character. The prideful soul will not allow it. No one will ever receive and benefit from discipling unless there is a depth of humility. Jesus told his closest friends that they would not even enter the kingdom of heaven, much less become great, unless they changed and humbled themselves (Matthew 18:1-4). There was no way that he could mold them into the kind of men they needed to be without humility.

Many of you reading this book have people in your life who are "discipling" you, mentoring you or counseling you. If you do not have this, it is most likely that you have been too self-sufficient and prideful to admit to anyone that you need it. However, those who have admitted that need must go deeper and ask, "Am I really taking advantage of this opportunity? Do I really have a humility of heart that enables me to learn and change as a result of the counsel and guidance I am receiving?" God gives grace to the humble in all situations, but this is never more true than in relationships whose purpose is to help us grow. Let me mention several ways humility should be demonstrated in such a relationship.

First, show respect and appreciation for those God has placed in your life. You need other people in your life. Admit it! Then be grateful they are there. Make them glad they get to help you. Make their work a joy, not a burden. Look for new and fresh ways to show your gratitude.

Second, get open very quickly and stay open. Do not make others have to dig and probe to find out where you really are.

Do not put up walls and cleverly designed barriers that keep people from knowing what is in your heart. Throw out the policy of "Don't tell, if they don't ask." Even if the friends helping you have not been as open with you as they ought to be, it is still right for you to be open with them. God will bless your humility.

Third, be eager to be submissive. Very few in the modern world would agree with this idea, but God's word says submission is good and wise (Ephesians 5:21ff; James 3:17; 1 Peter 2:18-3:8; 1 Peter 5:5-6). Yes, we must learn to think for ourselves. No, we must not blindly obey or submit to anyone. However, in the context of spiritual relationships in which no compromise of God's word is involved, we must trust that God will work through our submission. Even if the input we are given should turn out not to be the very best, God will bless our humble response to it. If someone who is trying to help us encourages us to read a certain book, study a certain passage, focus on a certain area of our lives or even take a certain challenge, humility calls for a real openness to submit to their input. Of course, if we feel that the advice we are given is unwise or is not Biblical, we should be true to our conscience. In such cases we should, with humility, express our concerns and talk the issue through to resolution. But, in my view, flouting the advice and just going out and doing something different is not being true to the Biblical idea of humility.

Fourth, listen carefully to input. James' words are most important:

> My dear brothers, take note of this: Everyone should be quick to listen, slow to speak and slow to become angry.... (James 1:19)

Give your mind and heart to understanding the counsel you are given. Drop all efforts to defend yourself. Don't interrupt and explain how the other person is wrong. If he or she is missing the mark, that will become evident without you having to be defensive. Listen, pray and seek to learn something about yourself. And then act on what you hear.

Fifth, seek advice. If you are known as an independent soul who often acts without seeking advice, your heart is not humble. The book of Proverbs is filled with admonitions about getting advice. It is the way of wisdom. We have seen some people become overly dependent on advice and become lazy when it comes to doing their own thinking; this, of course, is not the spirit that Proverbs is encouraging us to have. And honestly, this is not the problem most of us have. Also, there is nothing to limit you to getting advice from just one source. Just be sure that you are not simply trying to find someone who will agree with some conclusion to which you have already come. There is no humility in that!

We will all need discipling—that is, others helping us to be disciples of Jesus—as long as we live. I will never become so mature that I will no longer need the help of others. We can keep receiving that help only if we are humble.

Years ago, a critic of discipling wrote a paper entitled, "The Discipling Dilemma." Discipling, properly understood, is no dilemma at all when it is carried out with humility by all involved. When those helping others and those being helped are completely humble with one another, the results are relationships in which people are being changed into the image of Christ.

• **Thought Question** •

*When is the last time you asked someone
who is helping you to tell you how humble they find
you to be? When will you do it?*

chapter 11

humility and marriage

Roger Miller had several top ten hits in the 1960s. Most famous was his song "King of the Road," but the line from another hit is the one that I remember best: "Pride is the chief cause of the decline of the number of husbands and wives." That was almost prophetic. The divorce rate was just starting to climb in the '60s, and it would skyrocket in the 1970s. Miller was right. Pride was, and still is, the chief cause of the decline of the number of husbands and wives. And in those cases in which there is no divorce, pride is the chief cause of unhappiness.

Because I spend more time in my marriage than in any other relationship I have, it is the one place where I will face the most temptation to be prideful. I love my wife more than I love any other earthly person. That's the way God said it should be. But that doesn't mean all my struggles with pride got parked at the door when we married almost thirty years ago. She undoubtedly has seen more prideful responses from me than any other person. Because my pride is generally the quiet kind, some people are fooled. My wife is not; she knows me. If I am going to deal with pride in my life, I have to keep dealing with it at home, for *the way we are at home is the way we really are.*

I am not exaggerating at all when I say that earth's greatest blessings come to the husband and the wife who learn to show humility, first to God and then to one another. There is no marital challenge that cannot be overcome when humility resides in the hearts of a man and woman. Before Paul gets to the specifics about marriage in Ephesians 5, he gives us a word in Ephesians 4 that makes a powerful difference when applied in marriage:

> Be completely humble and gentle; be patient, bearing with one another in love. Make every effort to keep the unity of the Spirit through the bond of peace. (Ephesians 4:2-3)

In almost three decades of marriage, my wife and I have seen a lot of what life can throw at you, and we have had the normal share of bumps, hurts and misunderstandings. We have given each other a lot of love, but we have also caused each other some pain. But as we enter into our fifties, our marriage is better than ever. We still have our bumps (we haven't figured out how to be perfect!), and those bumps still bang us up emotionally, but we have learned at those times that we need to do two things, in this order: (1) stop and pray (that is, humble ourselves before God *together*), and then (2) confess our sin and forgive one another (that is, humble ourselves before each other). One hundred percent of the time that puts us on the road to healing and renewed happiness. In Christ, we are already unified, but pride keeps us from experiencing that which God has already given us. Before we humble ourselves, Sheila and I can feel miles apart, but humility allows the Spirit to bring us together—sometimes with amazing speed. When pride dies, the Spirit can bring his life-giving power.

There is no doubt that humility belongs in marriage. Seven is the number for perfection in ancient numerology, so in the rest of this chapter we will look at seven principles for practicing humility in marriage. Do not misunderstand. This will not give you a perfect marriage, but if you take each one of these seriously, you will enjoy a little foretaste of heaven on earth. Guaranteed.

1. Listen carefully when your spouse gives you input. We are assuming that you did not pick up this book and turn first to this chapter. We are assuming that you read all the things we have said about the basis and need for humility. Now we are saying: Practice what you have learned with the most important person in your life.

When you get input, sure, you will be tempted to be prideful (and start thinking immediately about all of his or her flaws that you know well), but fight the temptation. Be disciplined in your response. Yes, your partner can be wrong about you, but in most cases, no one knows you as well as your spouse, and there is likely to be some—if not a great deal of—truth in the input he or she is giving you.

2. Stop keeping score and being competitive. Realize that in a marriage, when one person wins, the marriage loses. So, do you really want to win? Don't keep up with how often he or she did something. "Love...keeps no record of wrongs" (1 Corinthians 13:5). Score keeping comes from a competitive spirit, and that spirit is born of pride. "Pride," says C. S. Lewis, "is competitive by its very nature, while other vices are competitive, so to speak, by accident."*

I don't know how often I have counseled couples in which one, or both, has a list of things, sometimes written, or more often just in their heads and hearts, that prove how bad the other person is. When you finish tearing down your marriage partner, what materials do you have left with which to build a strong marriage? Do we forget that building a strong marriage takes two people who feel loved and respected?

3. Welcome and seek input from outside your marriage. Following a thoroughly Biblical plan, every married couple will have other Christians in their lives who can give them wise counsel and encouragement. We all need this. I consider our marriage to be about as healthy as you will find (and my wife agrees), but we regularly ask for input from other mature couples who are in our lives. Marriage counseling is not just for those considering divorce. We have a standing rule that if either of us feels the need to get an objective opinion from a "third party," then it shall be done.

I know of cases in which husbands who are Christians have absolutely forbidden their wives to get help from outside the marriage. This is rooted completely in pride, and I have told husbands that they are in sin and that they will never give their wives a sense of being safe in their marriages (so important to women) until they humble out and welcome the input that is needed.

One final note on this point: When those who are helping you do give you Biblical input, do what they say and do it urgently. Don't argue with them or defend yourself and make excuses. Just humbly receive the Word and put it into practice. In fact, go the second mile. Do even more than they ask of you. Your marriage is worth it!

4. *Pray together daily.* We were still early in our marriage when I heard a man say: "Unless two people [in marriage] can fall on their knees and say together, '*Our* Father who is in heaven' that marriage is in trouble at the most basic level." In the same passage that this man referred to, Jesus taught us to pray, "Give us today our daily bread." Sounds like Jesus expected daily prayer. If a man and woman in marriage humble themselves before God every day and extol his "hallowed" name and ask that their needs—physical, emotional and spiritual—be met, their marriage will stay far away from trouble. They will have the normal bumps, but there will be a spiritual atmosphere in that marriage that enables all conflicts to be resolved. (Those of you who do not have Christian spouses may be wondering how all this applies to you. We will comment on this when we look at the last principle.)

5. *Apologize quickly and confess thoroughly.* The best of us (whoever that might be) will foul up. Combine the fact that we are still sinful creatures with the fact that we are frequently under pressure, and we will get plenty of mess ups. Most of those will have pride at their root.

We cannot totally eradicate sin. Nobody does. But what you can do is learn to recognize your sin and apologize for it quickly. And really we must go beyond apologizing to the more Biblical idea of confessing sin. My wife and I both found it hard to say, "I am sorry, but I sinned against you," but as we learned to do that, it had a healing effect. The party sinned against knew the other person was not minimizing what had happened.

It requires humility to say "I was being prideful," but that humility dramatically changes the atmosphere and leads to reconciliation and full resolution. Start saying this immediately every time you need to do so. (You will have plenty of opportunities!)

6. *Forgive completely.* The loop has not been closed, and the transaction has not been completed until the person sinned against says, "I forgive you." As we have seen in this book, asking for forgiveness requires humility—but so does giving it. The spouse who needs to forgive must stand at the foot of the cross and realize how much he or she has been forgiven, and then offer that same mercy to the other.

7. *Practice humility, even if your spouse does not.* Some of you are married to one who is not a Christian. Others of you are married to Christians who are not living as though they are. In either case the rule is the same: You do what is right. You live humbly before God and humbly before your spouse. Practice everything on this list. Get as much input as you can about how to handle your side of the marriage. If your spouse does not want to pray with you, pray by yourself for your marriage and for your partner. Go back and read the section on self-righteousness in chapter 9 and treat that form of pride like the plague in your life. You will be tempted to have it. Don't. This is the approach Peter is calling for when he writes to women whose husbands are not Christians:

> Wives, in the same way be submissive to your husbands so that, if any of them do not believe the word, they may be won over without words by the behavior of their wives, when they see the purity and reverence of your lives. Your beauty should not come from outward adornment, such as braided hair and the wearing of gold jewelry and fine clothes. Instead, it should be that of your inner self, the unfading beauty of a gentle and quiet spirit, which is of great worth in God's sight. (1 Peter 3:1-4)

This is just another passage reminding us of the power of humility. When we walk humbly with our God, he works in our lives and accomplishes what we cannot.

When a marriage is not going well, when there is no unity, when there is hurt and disappointment, be assured that there is a lack of humility. That lack of humility may start out in one person. It usually spreads to the other, but nothing will really get better until pride dies. Marriage was designed by God, and when we follow his plans, marriage is simply as good as it gets in this world. Nothing destroys marriage quicker than pride. Nothing causes it to flourish like humility.

• Thought Question •

What would your spouse say you most need to change in order to show humility in your marriage? Will you ask him/her?

NOTES

*C. S. Lewis, *Mere Christianity* (New York: Macmillan Publishing, 1943), 109.

chapter 12

humility and parenting

My wife, Terrie, and I have three girls. By the grace of God they are all faithful Christians and leaders among their peers. (Humility in parenting starts with a recognition that it is only by God's grace that this happens.) Often we are approached by others who want help with raising their children. Either problems have already begun in their families, or they just want direction before it is too late. These parents are doing the right thing. If there is anyone who needs to be especially humble, it is a parent.

It is hard to imagine an area of our lives that is more critical. I suspect that many of those who come to us do so knowing that the future of their family and the quality of their Christian experience for the rest of their lives is connected to how they raise their children. That thought can be overwhelming! There is this look in their eyes that says, "Just tell me three things to do so it all works out." I wish there were a three-point guide to raising children who will be faithful to God. But I do want all parents to understand that the number one person you can influence and change in your life is *you*. You are the one who needs to be changing the most if your children are going to faithfully follow Jesus. Nothing is more important as you raise your children than letting them see how God is making a difference in who you are. As we consider humility and parenting, let me offer several thoughts.

First, you must take personal responsibility for the raising of your children. There is nothing magical that happens just because you are in church. It is where you definitely need to be, but your children's faith and training are a charge given to you first and foremost. The Jews in Jeremiah's day had an unhealthy hope that the mere presence of the temple in Jerusalem would safeguard them from all attacks. Jeremiah's words are blunt:

> This is what the Lord Almighty, the God of Israel, says: Reform your ways and your actions, and I will let you live in this place. Do not trust in deceptive words and say, "This is the temple of the Lord, the temple of the Lord, the temple of the Lord!" If you really change your ways...then I will let you live in this place, in the land I gave your forefathers for ever and ever. But look, you are trusting in deceptive words that are worthless. (Jeremiah 7:3-8)

It is a humble, repentant heart that safeguards our lives, not merely being a member of God's church. Being in the church without teaching your children the importance of having the right heart (both with words and example) will not protect your family.

Our children, in most cases, are a reflection of who we are. Sure, there are some seeming exceptions, but in general our children become like us. If you say, "My child is out of control and won't listen to me," I must ask you questions like, "Who are you listening to? How are you as a disciple of Jesus? Does humility truly characterize your heart? Who taught them that you don't have to listen, really? Where did they learn that?" It is always important to consider the qualities that irk you in your children and then take a look to see if those qualities are in you. To change them requires changing *you* first.

Second, don't just welcome advice and counsel about parenting; seek it. Go after it like a starving man goes after food. As we have talked with other leaders, we have come to the conclusion that people may be more defensive about parenting than any area of their lives. What a tragedy! Guess who pays for that? A whole host of children.

> Listen to advice and accept instruction,
> and in the end you will be wise. (Proverbs 19:20)

There are still far too many parents who are too prideful to submit to this message. They seem to think that they will do what they think best and things will turn out fine. For a while it may seem to work out, but then their children hit the preteen and teen years, and it is a whole different story. Had they been getting advice all along, they could have had a different result. God would have blessed their humility.

You didn't ask because you were embarrassed? You didn't get input because you thought that the problems would just go away, that it was just a phase? You felt like such a failure and were so totally absorbed with self-pity that you didn't seek help? You didn't want to take the input because you felt protective for your children? The real problem is not the kids. The real problem is you, and the issue is pride.

God blesses the humble but "the LORD tears down the proud man's house" (Proverbs 15:25). Seek counsel and advice at every opportunity. Your children's teachers can be a valuable resource to you, especially those who teach your children in Bible classes. If your children spend the night at other Christians' homes, ask the parents if they saw areas in them that need work. Arrange family devotional times with those in your ministry so that they can see firsthand how your children are doing and how they are interacting.

Be proactive, not passive, not waiting for others to tell you what they think. If you are doing that, chances are, everyone senses the walls, and they are probably holding back. Absolutely no good comes from such behavior. You cannot change every situation, but you can change yourself. You can be humble! God is eager to bless and lift us up when we are just that!

Who have you received advice from about your parenting? How often do you get such advice? How often do you ask others for feedback and input? Are you known for having no defensiveness in this area at all? If you are looking for another powerful reason to crucify your pride, you have just found it, if you are a parent. Your son needs you to do that. Your daughter needs you to do that. If you do not humble yourself and get advice, counsel and help, they will suffer the consequences.

Third, work in a team effort with others. It has been well said that it takes a village to raise a child. Only a prideful and foolish parent says, "I can do it all by myself." Surround yourself with committed Christians. Paul describes how closely we are to work together as the family of God:

> Just as each of us has one body with many members, and these members do not all have the same function, so in Christ we who are many form one body, and each member belongs to all the others. (Romans 12:4-5)

Yes, your children are especially and uniquely yours. But in humility say, "our family belongs to all the others," and let these others into your life to help with this monumental task of raising children. There are others in the body of Christ who can do for your child things you cannot do. Let them help. All of us who have seen our children come through the teen years and grow to be strong Christians are deeply grateful for strong teen ministries and sacrificial workers in those ministries who invested hours into our children. We don't for a minute think we could have done it on our own. Many churches have strong preteen ministries now. Be thankful for the people who work in these ministries. Compare notes with them. Support them. Work in a partnership with them. You need them and your children need you to be united with them.

Fourth, make all attempts to not exasperate your children. This is very much connected to humility, because it means treating your children with consideration. Listen to the Scripture:

> Fathers, do not exasperate your children; instead, bring them up in the training and instruction of the Lord. (Ephesians 6:4)

There are many ways parents can frustrate their children. One clear way is for them to perceive from you that you are more worried about how they look to others than how they really are doing—that you are more concerned about what others think of you and your parenting than about what is really going on. This is an expression of pride on your part that your children will not fail to recognize. It exasperates them and instinctively moves them to rebellion.

Another way to exasperate your children is to refuse to ever be wrong. When we make mistakes, the thing that most destroys our credibility with our children is not the mistakes, but how we handle them. If we listen to our spouses or our friends or just become convicted by our own time with God, and then come back and humbly apologize to our children, the damage is usually reversed. Children love to forgive! But if we stubbornly insist that we were right or deny that there was any serious problem, we will very likely embitter a child and make it difficult for them to trust. No parent always does the right thing. Humility about our mistakes draws our children to us. Pride almost always causes a negative reaction.

There are some clear signs of this kind of pride in parents. For example one sign is a defensiveness about any criticism concerning their children. The response "I can't believe they acted that way; they are so good at home," is a good indication that one is proud and self-deceived. (By the way, the normal response of a healthy family to a comment about how "good" they were, is "Thanks, but we are still working on some things at home." That implies that discipling is an ongoing exercise and character is being taught.)

Finally, some things require much prayer. Parenting is one of those things. "He replied, 'This kind can come out only by prayer'" (Mark 9:29). In this text a young boy is totally out of control; the demons have him. Nobody can help and nothing works. Our children are not demon possessed, but the principle is true that much prayer is needed if they are to make it. It is beyond us, beyond our capabilities. We need help from God himself; we need supernatural intervention. We need wisdom that is far beyond our wisest thoughts. In other words, we need to be praying daily about the salvation of our children.

Every night from the time my children were little until they reached their teens, I would pray with them and over them with the request to God that one day they would become Christians and that they would one day marry *strong* Christians. I wanted them to hear that prayer request which I sincerely made to God daily.

Though I am convinced that the battle is really more with us than our children, there are some specific areas in child rearing that need our attention as we deal with pride in our children's lives as well. There are some critical areas to watch as pride rears its ugly head in our little ones.

First, be on guard against "haughty eyes." "Whoever has haughty eyes and a proud heart, him will I not endure" (Psalm 101:5b). "Haughty eyes and a proud heart, the lamp of the wicked, are sin!" (Proverbs 21:4). In this second verse, we see Hebrew parallelism being used for emphasis. "Haughty eyes" is parallel to the "lamp of the wicked." Haughty eyes isn't just an emotional response to authority or a mood swing, but that which reveals the heart of a person.

Jesus in Luke 11:34 describes our eyes as the lamp of our body. If they are good, the whole body is good, but if they are evil, the whole body is full of darkness. Haughty eyes reveal that evil and wickedness are finding their home in our children's lives. It would be hard to hear from someone that your child is wicked! But you need to listen to the word of God and take seriously its assessment of what is really going on in their heart. You have to be more concerned with their heart rather than mere compliance. They may do what you ask, but if their look and eyes are haughty, then you cannot settle for "peace, peace… when there is no peace"(Jeremiah 6:14). They have an attitude that has to change: Pride is present and rife.

We always made sure our children made eye contact as they listened to Terrie and me, or interacted with visitors. Their eyes reveal so much of their character. I wanted others to see their eyes and influence them or warn us if something seemed off.

Second, always deal with defensiveness. It is crucial that our children learn to take input and correction without having an emotional meltdown. Though we have to be careful that we are not harsh and oppressive, their ability to learn from correction will lead them to healthy spiritual growth.

Third, always teach your children to be servants. It is not enough that they serve you. Children serving their parents may be a "career move." They benefit from such behavior. Teaching them to serve their fellow Christians and other children and adults trains them in having a humble and giving spirit.

Our children become strong Christians in the same way we do—by the grace of God! But we receive that grace into our families by being spiritual and trusting his promises with a humble, childlike heart.

• Thought Question •

*How do your children know that you believe
deeply in the power of humility?*

chapter 13

humility in leadership

Scene One: It was an exciting day many years ago. I was being introduced as the lead evangelist of the church. The crowd was standing and applauding. All my dreams were being fulfilled. I was feeling awesome. It was an encouraging and satisfying moment!

Scene Two: My wife and I were overseeing several churches in the Midwest. We flew in to Michigan to meet with one of the churches and joined the staff for dinner at a Cajun restaurant, in deference to my Louisiana heritage. We walked into the restaurant to a spontaneous round of applause from the ministry staff. They warmly gathered around, wishing to meet any need. We were seated at the place of honor and asked if they could get us anything. They seemed to listen to every word, watching out of the corner of their eyes every movement and expression we made. They were so warm and appreciative. It was an encouraging and satisfying moment!

There is nothing wrong with scenes like these. They are respectful and healthy. But sin is always crouching at the door. While someone in such a crowd may be tempted with pride (in the form of envy or bitterness), the one who is perhaps tempted the most with pride is the leader himself.

Jesus' Message: Be a Servant

It is no wonder that Jesus twice addressed his disciples and several times illustrated to his men the essentiality of humility in leadership. The problem is simple: Leaders will always be tempted with pride and drawn toward worldly leadership styles. It comes with the turf. Being a disciple of Jesus does not make one immune to such temptation. Leaders, we are foolish if we do not openly admit that this is a problem which must be addressed.

> An argument started among the disciples as to which of them would be the greatest. Jesus, knowing their thoughts, took a little child and had him stand beside him. Then he said to them, "Whoever welcomes this little child in my name welcomes me; and whoever welcomes me welcomes the one who sent me. For he who is least among you all—he is the greatest." (Luke 9:46-48)

> When the ten heard about this, they became indignant with James and John. Jesus called them together and said, "You know that those who are regarded as rulers of the Gentiles lord it over them, and their high officials exercise authority over them. Not so with you. Instead, whoever wants to become great among you must be your servant, and whoever wants to be first must be slave of all." (Mark 10:41-44)

> Also a dispute arose among them as to which of them was considered to be greatest. Jesus said to them, "The kings of the Gentiles lord it over them; and those who exercise authority over them call themselves Benefactors. But you are not to be like that. Instead, the greatest among you should be like the youngest, and the one who rules like the one who serves. For who is greater, the one who is at the table or the one who serves? Is it not the one who is at the table? But I am among you as one who serves." (Luke 22:24-27)

Imagine a discussion as to who was the greatest. The "greatest" at what, I wonder? The greatest preacher, the greatest ministry grower, the greatest overall leader, the greatest mentor? Were they supporting themselves as the best candidates, or were there groups with their candidates versus other groups with their own? From our perspective it all looks so ridiculous. Why couldn't they just get along? When we sent out a survey to various leaders in the church asking the question, "Where do you see pride cropping up in your own life?" one common response was, "Being non-supportive, not outwardly getting behind peers, not celebrating their victories, not mourning their defeats and comforting and encouraging them, but rather, being highly competitive." We must commend them for their honesty, but their responses showed that not much has changed over the last two thousand years.

Jesus has some clear solutions that can help us as we strive both to lead and to stay humble.

First, we need to understand and take hold of the charge of Jesus to future leaders that "he who is least among you all—he is the greatest" (Luke 9:48b). Paul would later say of Jesus in Philippians 2:7 that he "made himself nothing, taking the very nature of a servant." Are you out to make yourself something or to make yourself nothing for the sake of the gospel? We can understand this principle, but to take hold of it is another question. When you test yourself in this area, the prideful results are easy to identify: wanting to hear your name publicly; wanting to be recognized by others at conferences; being overly concerned with titles; and being offended if not treated in a way equal to your "station" in the church. Most of us are too concerned about how our peers and those over us view us. It is so comical (and sad) at large meetings of Christians when I am so worried about how others view what I am doing, only to find out that most do not even remember where I live now! Probably, they are too busy worrying about what everyone is thinking of them. There has to be an effort on our part to fight our sinful nature as it tries to rear its ugly head in terms of leadership and its perks.

Second, Jesus emphasized and insisted that if one chooses to lead, he chooses to be a servant. We have already looked at the attitude of servanthood in general. Now we must apply it even more specifically to leaders. Nothing helps us to stay humble more than service. At every juncture when his disciples argued and were divided over "greatness," Jesus emphatically talked about being a servant, yes, even a slave, to those they led. Jesus himself served at the table, washed his disciples' feet and commands that we do likewise. If we want to lead people, we must serve those very same people.

Unfortunately Jesus' plan is not always carried out. For example, the leader wants others to learn to be servants, so he gets *them* to serve *him* in various ways. They in turn get others to learn servanthood by serving them. So service is learned by serving those who are our leaders—the opposite of what Jesus taught. There is nothing wrong in serving our leaders. In fact it is a great way to show our gratitude toward them for the time and effort they have spent helping us. Jesus did have his disciples make arrangements and do many organizational tasks. But the thrust of the Scriptures repeatedly is to make sure we serve those *we lead*. This is what makes us different from those in the secular or corporate world. This service needs to take the form of the mundane when that is the need.

Serving is more than just giving godly advice and leadership to people. When Jesus takes the towel and begins to wash feet and teaches us to do the same, he is talking quite specifically about leaders mundanely serving those they lead. The question everyone needs to ask is how often or regularly do I serve those I lead in that way? Do those I lead occasionally wash my car, clean my house or cut my lawn? There is absolutely nothing wrong with that, but have you occasionally and regularly served them in such ways? Serving our leaders can teach humility, but not necessarily. We may be attempting to win their approval. Serving those we lead brings our pride to the forefront and tests our willingness to be humble. This is the specific instruction Jesus gave his disciples when he saw them struggling with their pride in leadership. The leader who serves the people he leads gets their attention because there is nothing like that in the secular world. It is spiritual leadership modeled on Jesus who came not "to be served, but to serve, and to give his life as a ransom for many" (Mark 10:45), and it stands in contrast with worldly leadership.

Have a regular checklist as you guard your heart against pride, and aim to be "completely humble." How am I in the fellowship? Am I the first to slip out after I speak, or do I go around spending time with members and visitors, trying to meet as many needs as I can? When was the last time I served in a "foot-washing" manner? Am I concerned about who is greatest and where I rank in the pack? Am I regularly dealing with selfish ambition, not becoming morose about it, but constantly repenting and reminding myself that I am to make myself nothing and make Jesus everything? Do I give as much attention to the "less important" people in the fellowship as I do to the "more important"?

Leaders As Models of Humility

Leaders must model humility through service. This was the heart of Jesus' message. He who has ears, let him hear. But the Scriptures would call leaders to be examples of humility in other areas also.

First, every leader should work to be approachable. Jesus was the top leader. You do not get stronger or more powerful than he was. But the people did not think, "I should not talk to *him*" or "I don't think he would be interested in *me*" or "I think he would be bothered by children." Lepers came to him. A woman who was sick and destitute came. Prostitutes came, people brought their children, and men made a hole in a roof to bring their lame friend to him. Leaders, are you that approachable? Or is there something smug in your demeanor? Do you subtly or not so subtly communicate that you are too important for certain people? Are you always so surrounded by other leaders and more high-profile people that the average person feels intimidated trying to get to you? Where do you sit in an assembly? Only with the more important or with the less prominent? Dare you ask others to find out how approachable you are? The leader striving for humility will want to know.

Second, leaders should seek input and advice not just from other leaders but from those whom they lead as well. Other leaders will have one perspective, but the nonleader will often have a different, but equally valuable, viewpoint. We should leave no doubt among our people that we want to hear from them. Obviously, a leader cannot be getting feedback from everyone. He would never spend time doing anything else if that were his goal, but he should create an atmosphere in which such information can flow freely to him. Certainly what the people think is not always the deciding issue (just consider some of the things Moses heard), but good decisions cannot be made and the Scriptures cannot be applied wisely if we are not in touch with the feelings and thoughts of the people.

Finally, the leader should be the example of openness and confession. A worldly approach to leadership operates on the idea that you cannot lead if people know your weaknesses or your failures. In God's church there is an entirely different value system. But we can forget that the leader who will be the most respected will be the leader who is completely honest, forthcoming and vulnerable. Obviously, he or she should not use every setting to list shortcomings, but a leader should be known as one who brings where he or she really is out into the light. When confession is coupled with repentance and when repentance is clearly seen, credibility is gained, not lost.

Leadership is challenging. It brings many tests of the heart. If we become overwhelmed or overly introspective about motives and attitudes, we will do no good for anyone. However, if we keep our focus on Jesus and show a radical dependence on his grace, we can lead in ways that God will gloriously bless. The solution is not found in a once-and-for-all victory over our pride, but in the choice to stay in the battle, making every effort to be completely humble.

Scott Green, in a recent series of messages on spiritual leadership, uniquely characterized a similarity between proud and humble leaders. We conclude with his comment:

Proud leaders and humble leaders have something special in common: neither of them knows it. For the proud believe themselves sufficiently humble to get on with their "great things," while the humble—not falsely humble, which is self-disparagement, but genuinely humble of heart—believe themselves to be sufficiently proud to mandate more listening and learning. Both leaders are deceived, but which would you rather be, for they are heading in two very different directions! At journey's end, the proud will still be dithering around deluded; but the humble will have forged a special freedom, for they have forgotten about themselves entirely.*

• **Thought Question** •

*How do you attempt to model humility
for those you lead?*

NOTES

*Scott Green, "'The Worst of Sinners': The Power of Humility," in *Spiritual Leadership*, an audio series (Billerica, Mass.: DPI, 1998), cassette 2.

chapter 14

humility and 'followership'

The emphasis Jesus placed on humility when speaking to leaders should get the attention of the church—especially those who lead. But humility is to be all-pervasive in the body of Christ, and that means it should be found not only among leaders but among followers. Following may seem to imply humility, but we should not take that for granted.

The church is *a body*. It is an organism composed of many members (Romans 12:5) who must allow God to connect them and work through them in such a way that amazing things get done. However, those connections will not be made and will not stay in place without humility.

God has ordained leadership in his church (Ephesians 4:11). That is not surprising. Without leadership, no group of people can accomplish anything. The football team must have a coach; the army must have a general; the courtroom must have a judge; the classroom must have a teacher; the company must have a CEO; the country must have a president or prime minister. People who say they are opposed to organized religion should be asked what has ever been accomplished by disorganized religion. Anarchy is not known for its successes in any arena.

So in order for a group to function and make a positive impact, there must be leadership. God knows far better than we that leadership can be abused. No doubt, that's why there are so many strong things said to leaders in the Scriptures. God knows that godly leadership is essential. But there is a corollary to that idea. If leadership is essential, so is "followership."

Biblical Guidance

Many of us will lead; all of us will, in some setting, be followers. Humility in leadership is topic number one. Humility must start in leaders and be modeled by them. But then humility in followers is no less essential. And so the Biblical writers call us to humility in our relationships with leaders. In our day, when most everyone questions authority, when respect toward those who are older and more experienced is at an all-time low and when public leaders are the objects of ridicule, we need to hear clearly God's will. Consider three examples:

> Now we ask you, brothers, to respect those who work hard among you, who are over you in the Lord and who admonish you. (1 Thessalonians 5:12)

> Remember your leaders, who spoke the word of God to you. Consider the outcome of their way of life and imitate their faith. (Hebrews 13:7)

> Obey your leaders and submit to their authority. They keep watch over you as men who must give an account. Obey them so that their work will be a joy, not a burden, for that would be of no advantage to you. (Hebrews 13:17)

In these passages are three key ideas: respect, imitation and obedience. Each of these is an expression of humility in our relationship to leaders. Let's consider each for a moment.

1. Respect. When someone is over you, the natural thing is to want to be over them instead—or at least to not like it that anyone would be over you. The prideful soul chafes against the idea of anyone directing his life, and particularly at the idea of someone admonishing or correcting him. Of course, millions of people allow it—for a paycheck—but they may never make peace with the idea. The Bible calls us to look at the hard work of a leader—at the long hours, at the perseverance, at the pressure he or she faces—and to show respect. This respect is not to be given only when the leader is perfect, otherwise it would never be given. No, it is to be given to other imperfect people who have accepted the responsibility of leadership and are giving their hearts to it.

2. Imitation. Our world seems schizophrenic when it comes to imitation. People will tell you that they do not want to imitate anyone; they just want to be themselves. But then they read the latest magazines to find out what the cool people are doing so that they can imitate them. God has made us all different. We could not become just like each other even if we tried—though, no doubt, some have tried. We are each unique and special with a particular set of gifts, talents and personality. When I hear people say, "I want to be just like John" (or whomever), I usually appreciate the heart behind their statement, but I hope they realize that it is never God's intention that they become just like this other person. Having said that, we must say that imitation is godly and needed. In the case of our text, we are told to consider our leaders and imitate their faith. It is an act of humility to say "I see in this person who leads me a faith and a heart for God that I need and which I will imitate."

3. Obedience. If our world is ambivalent about imitation, it is almost dead set against obedience, at least in any kind of situation in which one does not have to do it to keep a job. The whole idea of obeying a leader is repugnant to many. And yet Scripture clearly says, "Obey your leaders." It has been pointed out that the Greek text here carries the idea of "be willing to be persuaded." In either case, we are talking about approaching a leader with a spirit of humility, with an eagerness to be an asset to his plans, and with a desire to bring joy to him in his leadership.

To relate to leaders with humility is showing respect, imitating the good and doing what the leaders are asking you to do (as long, of course, as it is not in conflict with the will of God as you understand it).

Practical Matters

Having looked at the spirit of humility we are to bring into the body as we interact with leaders, it would be useful to look at some practical examples in which humility is missing.

1. *Failing to take direction.* Leading a church, a large segment of the church or even a small group is no easy task. The leader's goal is to unite all the members. He or she has to try to cover different angles and meet different needs and coordinate a variety of issues. As followers, it is prideful and selfish to think, *I will just do it my way.* When we have an organ in the body that starts acting like that, we have a word for it: diseased. Those who act independently are showing no concern for unity, and they are certainly showing no concern for the leader that God has placed before the group. While the leader's direction is not inspired or infallible, ignoring what a leader has said is an act of arrogance. It will bring harm to the person and harm to those to whom he is connected. If we have a legitimate concern about the direction given, we need to talk that through with a leader, but there is no humility in just doing what we would rather do.

2. *Withholding support from leaders.* Sometimes, because of pride and envy or just indifference, people will withhold support from their leaders. They will show no enthusiasm for plans. They will offer little that will help move those plans forward. A response like that communicates to others, "I don't approve" or "If they would let me plan this, I would come up with something better." Certainly, there are times when we have to go talk over something with a leader. Perhaps there is something about his plan that we cannot, in good conscience, get behind. But in such cases, our desire should be to settle matters quickly and to become completely united. *The humble heart will be eager to support a leader* and will want to remove any barriers to that support as quickly as possible.

3. *Second-guessing leaders.* There is a style of "followership" in which the person sits back, watches, gets involved to some degree, but then says later, "I knew that was not going to work"

or "I had serious doubts about that all along." Most of us have either done that or been strongly tempted to respond in that way. In that situation, we were withholding our heart and our commitment, and we may very well have contributed to the failure with our desire to be proven right.

A variation of this occurs when we do voice a concern up front, and then down the line somewhere, other leaders realize that what we said was right. At that point we can be thankful that what we saw finally came into the light, or we can be prideful and decide that things would be a lot better if we were just calling the shots all the time. We can let that one situation lead us to be distrustful of leadership and arrogant about our superior insight. You do not have to guess how much good that will do the church.

Anyone who has been in the church for much time at all has probably been hurt by a leader. This is not because most leaders are harsh or insensitive, but because everyone makes mistakes, and sooner or later something may happen that stings us or leaves us disillusioned. It is so important in those times not to give up on leadership or to give in to any of the attitudes we just described. Every effort should be made to resolve a grievance that we have, but whatever happens, it will always be God's will for us to work humbly with those who are raised up to lead.

We have every reason to expect leaders to be humble. But in the church we have every reason to expect followers to have that same humility. If we lose humility at either point, the body of Christ will be torn in two, and the evangelization of the world will have to wait for those who listen to Jesus more carefully than we do. However, when leaders and followers together are completely humble in their relationships with each other, God is able to do through us more than we can ask or imagine. The world will be changed by humble disciples of Jesus who lead and humble disciples of Jesus who follow.

• **Thought Question** •

Do you have the reputation of being a humble follower? If the answer is no, how much does that concern you?

part three

**humility
and
life**

chapter 15

humility in suffering

Imagine that you have committed yourself to God and have for years sought to walk with him and live in his ways. Then illness befalls you. You are chastened on a bed of pain. You have constant distress in your bones. You find food repulsive. Your soul loathes the choicest of foods. Your flesh begins to waste away. Your bones, once concealed under healthy flesh and muscle, now protrude. It is difficult for your family and friends to look upon you. This description of suffering is found in what may be the Bible's oldest book, the book of Job (33:19-22).

Or imagine that you have made the decision to follow Jesus Christ, but in the country where you live, that decision is not welcomed and not tolerated. Your property is confiscated. You are excluded from the community. Your parents hate you for what you have done. You are eventually arrested, tortured and placed in prison. Some of your brothers in the faith are killed and even dismembered. Such things have happened. The Bible refers to them all (see Matthew 10:21-22, Hebrews 10:34, John 16:2, Hebrews 11:35-37). Some of them are happening to Christians even as we write. How does one respond when such things take place? What do such things as these, and dozens of forms of suffering, have to do with pride and humility? A more careful look at Job's story can give us some valuable insights.

Satan's Attack

Satan argued to God that Job was a blameless and upright man, primarily because everything was going well in his life. After all he had had seven sons and three daughters, seven thousand sheep, three thousand camels, five hundred yoke of oxen, five hundred donkeys and a large number of servants. He was considered the greatest man among all the people of the East. Beyond that, his children just had one party after another (Job 1:2-4). In our day Job might have owned several large companies, a great deal of stock, a private plane and a place in Aspen. His children would have been known for their style. "Sure, he has a great attitude," argued Satan. "Everything is great."

And so God allowed Satan to afflict Job. The results of the early battles must have discouraged the enemy. All in one day Job's oxen and donkeys were stolen, his sheep and servants were struck by lightening, and all died, save one. His camels were stolen, and the servants caring for them were all slashed to death, save one. A violent windstorm struck the house where all his sons and daughters were having a party, and they all died (Job 1:13-19). And then we read:

> At this, Job got up and tore his robe and shaved his head. Then he fell to the ground in worship and said:
>
> "Naked I came from my mother's womb,
>   and naked I will depart.
> The Lord gave and the Lord has taken away;
>   may the name of the Lord be praised."
> In all this, Job did not sin by charging God with
>   wrongdoing. (Job 1:20-22)

With a remarkable humility and a remarkable faith, Job accepted the suffering. He did not understand it. His pain was certainly not eased, but he bowed before God, and in so many words said, "I still trust you."

The Pain Intensifies

But then the enemy turned up the heat. Job's internal suffering was now matched by the external kind. Painful sores covered him from head to toe. Such was his agony that he sat in ashes and scraped himself with broken pottery (Job 2:7-8). But it still looked as though he would pass the test. He got no help from a wife who would never make the faith Hall of Fame. Her advice (apparently given because it would be better for him *and* better for her): "Curse God and die." But Job was proving to be a formidable opponent, staying humble in the storms of life:

> He replied, "You are talking like a foolish woman. Shall we accept good from God, and not trouble?"
> In all this, Job did not sin in what he said. (Job 2:10)

However, as the suffering wore on day after day, it began to take its toll, and finally Job cursed the day of his birth. He did not fully take his wife's advice, but he did start down the road toward bitterness. Hours of discussions with friends followed, but Job eventually took the position that God was most unfair, and he protested vehemently to his Maker. Typical is this line from 7:11:

> "Therefore I will not keep silent;
> I will speak out in the anguish of my spirit,
> I will complain in the bitterness of my soul."

Let me ask you to think about something. How do you react to Job's situation? Do you think it was inevitable that he would come to this point? Do you think: *That is certainly the way I would have reacted?* Do you so identify with Job's suffering that you, too, begin to question God?

This is definitely the effect that suffering has on us. In the midst of suffering, it is not uncommon for us to feel that we certainly know better than God what ought to be done. Our pain rivets our attention inward. We cry out for relief. We cannot understand how a powerful and loving God would allow us to stay at this point.

When my first major multiple sclerosis (MS) attack came eight years ago, like Job, I did rather well in the early going, but then as the effects of the illness wore on me day after day, and I considered the years of challenge that were before me, I questioned if I wanted to live. It is remarkable to me now that I felt this way, but that is where I was at the time. From when I got up to when I went to sleep, it was difficult for me not to be consumed with my illness. Even my sleep was no longer normal. It was a twenty-four-hour-a-day problem. My heart and my faith were tested.

Coming Back to God

But you must not feel sorry for me, or for Job, or for thousands of people facing all kinds of trials and different forms of suffering—physical or emotional. God is still faithful. And he has not lost control. In his early response, Job was on track:

> "Naked I came from my mother's womb,
>   and naked I will depart.
> The Lord gave and the Lord has taken away;
>   may the name of the Lord be praised." (Job 1:20)

In the face of his suffering, he acknowledged two things:

1. God is still God. God has always been. He was there long before Job and long before Job's situation developed, and nothing that happens in any of our lives changes the reality of God or the nature of his character. It is interesting how some of us will have faith in him even though we live in a suffering-filled world. But as soon as that suffering comes under *our* roof, we doubt God or his faithfulness. Do we somehow think that what happens to us changes something about God?

2. Man is still the dependent, precarious human being he has always been. "Naked I came…and naked I will depart." Job knew that, even if he was the richest man in the East, he was still as the grass and the wildflowers: Here today and gone tomorrow.

And then Job did something else: *He praised God.* Sure, this is easier to do when all is well with us. When I wrote the first draft of this chapter, I was at a beautiful spot in northern New England where I like to go when isolation is needed. The water in front of the house was glassy, reflecting the mountains. It was an idyllic scene. The temperature was perfect. I had just eaten some delicious lasagna my wife had sent along. I felt relatively good that day, physically. A phone call had confirmed that a recently made decision was working out well. It was easy to give praise to God.

Today, as I make some revisions to this chapter, several people close to me are in a lot of pain and are, like Job, mystified by what they are going through. It has rained for four days straight with more predicted. The offices of seven of our staff members have flooded. That decision I referred to, which was made earlier, now appears to not be working out after all.

The truth is that today presents me a greater opportunity to show humility than that perfect day two months ago. When we suffer, we find out where we really are, and we learn lessons we never learned while all was comfortable. If our humility cannot pass the test of suffering, wasn't it just a disguise? Isn't it better that we find that out before it is too late to do something about it? If we say, "I don't deserve this kind of pain," we should stop and listen, and learn something very important about ourselves. We are a long way from the cross, a long way from dying to self. Our suffering has revealed that we are much more self-absorbed than we have thought. Nothing confronts us with our true selves like suffering. Suffering exposes the self-righteousness, arrogance and ingratitude that has been lodging somewhere in the recesses of our hearts. Suffering does not produce these things. It only reveals what is already there. No wonder God allows us to go through some tough things.

The truly humble person, the person who stands in awe before God, will make it through the tests of suffering and be stronger on the other side. He may struggle and wrestle with God, but ultimately, he will come back to God in full surrender like Job did:

> Then Job replied to the Lord:
>
> "I know that you can do all things;
> no plan of yours can be thwarted.
> You asked, 'Who is this that obscures my
> counsel without knowledge?'
> Surely I spoke of things I did not understand,
> things too wonderful for me to know." (Job 42:1-3)

Years ago I heard a man talk about King David and all of his ups and downs. He said that while David made his share of mistakes, his redeeming character trait was *spiritual allegiance*. No matter what he went through or how many times he failed, he always came back to God. And that is what Job did. He had his good moments and then a lot of bad ones. The man who looked faithful and humble at first just overflowed with self-righteousness and bitterness later. But in the end he was humble. He stopped blaming and accusing God, and he said, "I spoke too soon. I said too much." As he humbled himself, he once again saw the blessings of God.

To humble ourselves in our suffering means to accept that suffering and allow God to teach us any lesson that we need to learn (and there will usually be several).

There is an old saying that goes like this: "Difficulty is the very atmosphere of miracle." None of us welcomes suffering. Few of us are immediately or consistently humble in the face of it. However, if we will come to God in our pain with teachable and open hearts, we may yet see miracles.

▪ Thought Question ▪

*What has suffering taught you
about your own heart?*

chapter 16

humility and convictions

Is there any pride worse than religious pride? Jesus came into a first-century world not unlike ours where there were various sects with differing doctrinal positions. Those who held those positions often did so in prideful ways. Jesus took note of this and challenged them:

> To some who were confident of their own righteousness and looked down on everybody else, Jesus told this parable. (Luke 18:9)

Ironically, while most religions extol humility, the most religious people in history have not been known as the most humble. Man's tendency is not just to believe things, but to believe them in ways that are arrogant, defensive, closed-minded and most of all, self-righteous. Religious pride, sadly, may be the most common of all of pride's manifestations and the most difficult from which to break free.

> "Be careful," Jesus said to them. "Be on your guard against the yeast of the Pharisees and Sadducees." (Matthew 16:6)

What Jesus was warning his disciples about was not just some incorrect teaching on the part of these sectarians. Particularly in the case of the Pharisees, much of what they taught was correct (Matthew 23:3). He was warning them about an attitude, an attitude that worked like yeast and spread into the lives of others. The Pharisees may have been the most zealous and even the most "evangelistic" of all the groups in Palestine, but Jesus was not impressed:

> "Woe to you, teachers of the law and Pharisees, you hypocrites! You travel over land and sea to win a single convert, and when he becomes one, you make him twice as much a son of hell as you are." (Matthew 23:15)

The Pharisees took care of all the details, strictly observing the Sabbath and all the rules about tithing. But Jesus saw that something deeper and more important was missing:

> "Woe to you Pharisees, because you give God a tenth of your mint, rue and all other kinds of garden herbs, but you neglect justice and the love of God. You should have practiced the latter without leaving the former undone." (Luke 11:42)

These men were devoted to their religion. They were held in high esteem by the average person, but Jesus saw the pride beneath their flowing robes and phylacteries (little boxes attached to their robes which held portions of Scripture):

> "Everything they do is done for men to see: They make their phylacteries wide and the tassels on their garments long; they love the place of honor at banquets and the most important seats in the synagogues; they love to be greeted in the marketplaces and to have men call them 'Rabbi.'" (Matthew 23:5-7)

Now, the worst thing in the world we can do is to look down on these Pharisees and say, "I thank you, Lord, that I am not like these Pharisees" (compare Luke 18:11). They were not the most sinful men ever to live. Their tendencies were fairly normal and can be found throughout history. They are caricatures of what we all can be. There is not a one of us who is not tempted to be like them at various points. I dare say we have all manifested attitudes just like theirs at some time. To say, "Oh, I would never be like a Pharisee" is to be just like them!

Though they have been the subject of many a joke and story, we can be thankful that the Pharisees were active during the time of Jesus, for they show us in the clearest way what religious pride looks like. In light of their example, we must face and find ways to meet this great challenge: *how to be men and women of deep conviction and at the same time, to have true humility.*

A Difficult Challenge

We must realize, going into it, that this is no easy task. As soon as we align ourselves with the truth, the sin of religious pride crouches at the door wanting to have us (see Genesis 4:7). To combine conviction with humility will require us to remember everything we have learned so far about how a prideful soul can become humble, and most of all it will require the greatest dependence on the grace of God. Our first mistake is often to be overconfident and to think we can handle this issue on our own. The enemy laughs.

As noted in chapter 2, all freedom comes as a result of finding truth (John 8:32), and so, if this is going to be as difficult as we have indicated, we need all the truth we can find. There are several truths we must consider:

1. *The more convinced we are of our position, the more tempted we will be to look down on those who do not hold it.* We need deep convictions. Shallow convictions are hardly better than none at all. But our wholehearted commitment to something makes us immediately vulnerable to pride. As soon as we leave the worldly perspective and commit ourselves to being Christians, we can so quickly forget that the new birth happened solely by grace (see 1 Corinthians 15:10, Ephesians 2:5). We can begin to compare ourselves to other religious people who have shallow convictions and little commitment, and we can do what our friends the Pharisees did—be confident in our own righteousness and look down on everyone else. Having deep

convictions is not optional, but we must face the truth that this will create a temptation that many never overcome.

At one point in his life Paul was given some exceedingly great revelations. He says they came after he was "caught up to the third heaven" (2 Corinthians 12:2). But apparently God knew that gaining those new understandings could cause Paul to become prideful. So Paul writes:

> To keep me from becoming conceited because of these surpassingly great revelations, there was given me a thorn in my flesh, a messenger of Satan, to torment me. (2 Corinthians 12:7)

Let your mind stay on this phrase for a few moments: "to keep me from becoming conceited." It reminds us that even a spiritual warrior and fearless proclaimer of God's grace was vulnerable to spiritual pride. Knowing this, God sent something to help Paul stay humble. But the point should not be lost on us. As we gain deeper insights into grace, discipleship and the mysteries of the kingdom of God, we too will be tempted with spiritual pride. In many cases it has already become more than temptation.

2. *The longer we have held to a certain position or belief, the more difficult it will be for us to humbly be open to God for new insights.* And yet, humility before God and his word means we must always be longing to learn new truth. This definitely sets up a tension.

Longevity in a group that believes certain doctrines to be true can mean that we are getting much of our identity from being a part of that group. When that happens, a certain fear of losing our identity takes hold, and it becomes very difficult for us to consider that anything other than what we have believed could possibly be true. You have probably thought at some time or another: "What would happen if I came to a conviction that our group is wrong about some things?" If you have been a part of this spiritual community for at least five years, it is a painful thought. In fact, it is too painful for some people, and they shut the door to understanding further truth. It all becomes even more complicated when one is a leader and has an image, or a salary and a retirement fund to protect.

John's gospel gives us two examples of people making decisions because of fear of losing their place in their spiritual community:

> His parents said this because they were afraid of the Jews, for already the Jews had decided that anyone who acknowledged that Jesus was the Christ would be put out of the synagogue. (John 9:22)

> Yet at the same time many even among the leaders believed in him. But because of the Pharisees they would not confess their faith for fear they would be put out of the synagogue. (John 12:42)

Here we have people who perfectly illustrate our point. These people saw the truth of God in human flesh, but they dared not acknowledge it because their identity as Jews was tied up in their participation in the synagogue community. Some combination of fear and pride caused them to hold on to those relationships and not confess faith in Christ. If you are tempted to say, "Poor souls; that was an awful dilemma to put them in," remember that there were others who humbled themselves before the truth of God, accepted Christ and were put out of the synagogue (John 16:2). It was not an impossible situation, for they were chosen by Christ and he was with them (John 15:16).

What we are saying is that we must face the truth that long-held ideas are the hardest to give up. Thankfully, most of the ideas we hold to will never need to be given up, but we must stay open to what God wants to teach us, whatever the costs. This is true humility.

3. *The more convinced you are that you know how God's system works, the more difficult it will be for you to accept God's work that appears to you to be outside that system.* Here the

dilemma deepens. We need deep and passionate convictions about what Scripture teaches, but when we become convinced that God could never work outside our understanding of Scripture, we are no longer in a humble position. We have made *our understanding* of God's truth and *God's truth* one and the same, and this is a dangerous thing. Again, look at our friends the Pharisees:

> Some of the Pharisees said, "This man is not from God, for he does not keep the Sabbath."
> But others asked, "How can a sinner do such miraculous signs?" So they were divided. (John 9:16)

Their convictions about the Sabbath were deep, as is still true among the ultraorthodox in Israel today. Don't disparage that conviction. It was rooted in Scripture. But that conviction obscured their view of the larger work of God. In their minds, it was simple: Jesus could not possibly be from God because he did not keep the Sabbath—at least not in the way *they thought* one was supposed to keep the Sabbath.

In a religious debate, they could have defended their view of the Sabbath. Scripture might have appeared to be on their side. In their minds, they saw the plan of God, and in their minds, no work of God could go on outside the plan as they conceived it—a prideful posture. Jesus offered another perspective on the Sabbath, a higher and superior view (Mark 2:27-28), but they would not accept it. They knew how God worked, and what Jesus was doing did not fit that picture.

Can we make the same mistake? You don't think so? Then you are a Pharisee. Of course we can make it! We can make every mistake they made. That's why the Bible tells us so much about them—to warn us.

The original twelve disciples were not Pharisees. They came from a very different strata of the Jewish culture, but they had not been with Jesus very long before they had the same problem as their Pharisee brothers. Read what Luke describes:

> "Master," said John, "we saw a man driving out demons in your name and we tried to stop him, because he is not one of us."
> "Do not stop him," Jesus said, "for whoever is not against you is for you." (Luke 9:49-50)

"Not one of us." In a very short amount of time they had, to their satisfaction, figured out how God worked and with whom he worked. This man did not fit the profile as they saw it, and so they concluded that he could not be of God. Have you ever wondered why the gospel writers tell us this story?

4. *Some spiritual convictions do not come so much from careful Bible study as from the fact that we have heard something over and over.* Have you ever noticed that when something is repeated frequently and not challenged, it comes to be accepted as sacred truth? Humility before God's word means we will always be willing to reexamine our beliefs in light of Scripture—making sure they are rooted in the Bible and not just tradition. There is no way of knowing how many times Revelation 3:20 has been used to tell people how to become Christians. In that passage Jesus says:

> "Here I am! I stand at the door and knock. If anyone hears my voice and opens the door, I will come in and eat with him, and he with me."

Over and over, people in a variety of traditions have heard that this is all that is needed to become a Christian: Just open the door and receive Christ. It has become a part of the creed of untold millions. But a closer look reveals that this passage was written to people who had long been Christians. They were not in need of the new birth. In fact, they had already been reborn, had drifted away and were in need of repentance (v19). But after thousands of repetitions, many people would find it difficult to be humble before God's word and to study what Scripture actually teaches about how to be born again.

Watch out for religious pride. If this example does not apply to you, there is probably another one that does. Some of us, for example, have often heard that 2 Peter 1:20-21 teaches that nothing in Scripture is open to man's private interpretation, and we have used this passage to tell others that they must not interpret Scripture, but just read it and believe it. The passage says:

> Above all, you must understand that no prophecy of Scripture came about by the prophet's own interpretation. For prophecy never had its origin in the will of man, but men spoke from God as they were carried along by the Holy Spirit.

Do you see what I see? The passage does not say anything about *our* interpretation of Scripture. It says that the prophets who wrote Scripture did not come up with these words by *their own* interpretation. Instead, they were carried along by God's Spirit, and thus wrote what God wanted written. But again, I know that many people have heard this "wrong" *interpretation* of this passage so many times that they have accepted it as true. Do you see the irony? God must laugh at us. Or maybe he cries.

The challenging thought is that these are not the only two examples we could give. On other points we believe something because we have often heard it repeated rather than because it has a Biblical foundation. In humility, we must admit this.

Resolving the Dilemma

So we have a dilemma. We need deep convictions. We need to be men and women who have studied the Scriptures and see what is right and what is wrong. Then we need to preach and teach those things to others (1 Timothy 4:11). But at the same time we must be humble and watch out for the spiritual pride that can so easily come to those who are passionate and committed.

This is a challenge and one many people avoid by going to one extreme or the other. Some people just opt for the conviction side. They become Pharisees. They stand up for their convictions, but they get locked in and cannot see any new truth. Others opt for the "we can't really know anything, so let's just be tolerant of everything" attitude. In New England, where I have lived for ten years, you can just pick a church out of the phone book and likely this is precisely the attitude you will find.

So what is the answer? It is going to sound too simple: The answer is humility *before* God and faith *in* God. He allows us to experience many dilemmas and many tensions in life, and I am convinced he does it to cause us to depend on him more than ever.

It is not easy to be a man or woman of deep conviction who is at the same time always open to learning something new and always open to changing one's mind if shown a more correct way. But since it is God's will that we be both of these, it absolutely can be done. It will just require the greatest humility before God and great faith that he will provide the direction we need.

I know that for most readers of this book, the greatest challenge is to be open to new ideas. We have a fear that this will somehow cause us to soften the strong message of discipleship and commitment.

But think about this: If we had not been humble, we would never have been willing to accept the things we now believe about being disciples of Jesus. But such humility must never end. It can theoretically end when we have learned everything that we need to learn—when every idea and concept is just as God sees it. Obviously, that experience will not come in our lifetimes.

So the answer is to fearlessly teach what you believe to as many people as you can find, and at the same time, keep an Apollos-type openness that is ready to be refined, corrected or redirected (Acts 18:24-26). Humility says, "There is much more we all have to learn."

▪ Thought Question ▪

Do you have any fears about being humble in regard to new truth? Why must you not surrender to those?

chapter 17

humility in success and failure

Case One: The ministry took a downward turn. Low attendance, more problems and weak Christians were the only report. All the vital signs looked bad. What was going on? Well, I had a ton of excuses. "It is different where I live." "We don't have the right people on staff." "We need financial help." "I inherited the problems; they weren't mine but the previous evangelist's mistakes." I had a lot of excuses, but my pride kept me from admitting the problems and accepting responsibility.

Case Two: The ministry was going great. Attendance was outstanding. I had a few problems, but with the steady growth, we were fixing things. Our contribution met all the needs and more. My staff was admired by many! I was doing a great job! I was feeling a lot of things, but not necessarily humility.

These opposite-looking scenarios have a striking similarity: In both cases the personal pronouns, *I, my,* and *mine* are prominent. It is not just the bad times that give us a wake-up call and refine our hearts, but the good times are an equal test and refinement of our heart as well.

> The crucible for silver and the furnace for gold,
> but man is tested by the praise he receives
> (Proverbs 27:21).

The teaching of the Scriptures is clear: Failures and successes both test our hearts. They both reveal what we are really depending on. We can be full of pride or humility in one as well as the other.

Humility in Success

The story of King Hezekiah, found in both Isaiah 36-39 and 2 Kings 18-20, shows us a man who failed to stay humble when the blessings came. After initially humbling himself before God and praying a moving and seemingly sincere prayer, recorded in Isaiah 38:14-19, Hezekiah, and the nation of Judah, eventually enjoyed great success and prosperity. Following the success, however, Babylonian envoys paid Hezekiah a visit, having heard about all that God had done. The Chronicler describes what happened:

> But when envoys were sent by the rulers of Babylon to ask him about the miraculous sign that had occurred in the land, *God left him to test him* and to know *everything that was in his heart.* (2 Chronicles 32:31, emphasis added)

If we go to Isaiah's account (39:1-8) we see that "what was in his heart" was pride. He showed these guests his storehouse, his treasures and his palace. They had come to hear about God, and Hezekiah showed them what he (Hezekiah) had accomplished. When Hezekiah should have been giving glory to God, it appears that he was just making himself look good. Judging from Isaiah's conversation with Hezekiah, it was a bragging, boastful session with which the prophet and his God were not pleased.

When he is told by Isaiah that after his death judgment will come because of his actions, his response reveals the depth of his heart problem. He is told that everything he bragged about will end up in Babylon, and some of his own children will end up as eunuchs in the palace of the King of Babylon. His response is, "Fine, as long as there is peace in my lifetime." Imagine that! Some of his own flesh and blood will become eunuchs and slaves in Babylon, and his response is, "Well, as long as it doesn't happen to me." Can we become so self-centered and prideful that all we care about is ourselves and not the church and our children? The answer is yes!

Success may be a greater test of our pride than failure. It seems we humans have no trouble taking the credit for victory. We just feel so proud of what is happening! And that healthy pride so easily slides over to the unhealthy personal pride that God condemns. How do we stay humble in success?

First, give God the glory! Boasting about what we have done is universally condemned in Scripture. What we report and how we report it needs to be thought through, and our hearts need to be checked. While there is an unhealthy fear of pride that causes some to become paranoid about sharing anything, it is always wise to make sure God is our boast.

Second, in times of success, more than even times of defeat, we should spend more time in prayer and confession, not less. Often it is the times of defeat that motivate us to seek God's help and purify our lives. But what do we do in times of success? It is a powerful test. As with Hezekiah, God is watching to see everything in our hearts. Does he find us turning our eyes away from him and on to ourselves?

Third, in times of success we need to fix our eyes more intently on Jesus and his ministry and his character. In moments of great success, we will realize how we still fall far short of his glory and life. We will be humbled and challenged to take things higher. In our times of success, we must ask who is being lifted up and who is being glorified. Is it the risen Christ or that rascal self?

Humility in Failure

Humility in failure is not a given. We see people make mistakes that lead to failure and then turn right around and make the same mistakes again. Often our reaction to defeat and loss is prideful. We become angry with our circumstances, blame others or fall into self-pity, which is pride in disguise. King David had his many successes, but there were other times of defeat. While Hezekiah shows us pride in success, David can teach us how to be humble in failure.

At one point David had been relentlessly pursued by Saul. In despair David decides to flee to the enemy's camp to find peace:

> But David thought to himself, "One of these days I will be destroyed by the hand of Saul. The best thing I can do is to escape to the land of the Philistines. Then Saul will give up searching for me anywhere in Israel, and I will slip out of his hand." (1 Samuel 27:1)

David's counsel that he gave himself actually worked for a while. Saul did give up. But this "counsel" was not God reliant but man centered. "David thought to himself" was not exactly the phrase of the godly man who seeks God's will. There seemed to be peace until the moment that David found himself about to have to go to battle with the Philistines against King Saul himself. God saved him from this unrighteousness when some of the Philistine leaders did not wholly trust David (1 Samuel 29:4).

So David is spared to return to his home in Ziklag, only to find that the whole town has been raided and all their families and possessions are gone. In the midst of this horrific scene, David's men grow bitter and talk of stoning him (1 Samuel 30:6). This time, rather than "thinking to himself," David turns to God. In a very non-Rambo act, he calls for Abiathar the priest to bring the ephod to determine God's will. David's prayer is clear: "David inquired of the LORD, 'Shall I pursue this raiding party? Will I overtake them?'" The answer from God is equally clear: "Pursue them," he answered. "You will certainly overtake them and succeed in the rescue." And indeed he did.

In times of defeat, we must focus not on blaming, but on learning. We must guard against both self-defense and self-pity. The humble man says, "How can I grow from this, and how can I do better the next time?" The prideful man is worried about how he looks, about what others will think or what defense he can present. We must see a defeat as a great opportunity to depend more on God. We must renew our focus at those times on God's purposes, not on our pain.

The enemy is always looking for a way to get pride into our hearts. Success opens the door wide. Failure may present more of a challenge. But of this we can be sure: Whether we are up or whether we are down, the enemy has a plan to get us to rely on our own thinking, to blame someone else for our defeat and to take all the credit for the victories. A man is tested by the praise he receives, and he is tested by the losses he experiences. If we keep our eyes focused on God, we can stay humble when we lose and when we win.

• Thought Question •

*Write down a success and a failure
you had in the last year. What did you learn about
showing humility in both of these?*

chapter 18

humility and talent

Why is anyone given a talent—the ability to sing, to run, to speak, to write, to organize, to administer, to make money? Some people think the answer to all of these is always related to the last one—*to make money*. But there is another answer: to bring glory to God and accomplish his purposes. The fact that few people use their talents in this way does not change the reason for having them.

All talent is a gift. Sure, some people have worked hard to develop those talents, but that does not change the fact that what they started with was a gift: something they received freely, something they did not earn or deserve. Because talent is a gift, we all owe someone thanks for whatever talent we may have. (Christians know exactly who that is.) Because all talent is a gift, it is silly, foolish or both to be the least bit prideful about the talent we have. Should we get satisfaction from our talent? Absolutely. Should we feel superior to others because we have it? Absolutely not.

But the truth is, we often do feel superior. Or, on the other end of the spectrum, some of us feel inferior because we compare our gift to someone else's. This is why most everyone needs this chapter in some way.

What Humility Will Not Mean

We have already looked at some of the misconceptions about humility in chapter 7. Now it is time to look at another one:

Humility does not in any way mean that you will hide your talent or pretend that you do not have it. Going back to the foundation of this entire study, humility means standing in awe of God and wanting to please him. If God gave you a gift (and he gives gifts to everyone), then he certainly did not intend for you to put some kind of cowed look on your face and say, "I really can't do that." This is not humility because this is not gratitude. This is not humility because this is not submission to the God who gave you a gift as a part of a divine plan. This is not humility because this is not eagerness to serve. Responses like this are what give humility a bad name.

Paul recognized that he had various gifts of preaching, teaching and leadership. He would say, "I am the worst of sinners" or "I don't deserve to be called an apostle," because he knew that none of us deserves God's grace. However, he never held back from using those gifts that God had given him. In fact, he said "Woe to me if I do not preach the gospel!" (1 Corinthians 9:16). Paul believed that his life and all he was could be described as a gift. He also believed Jesus' message:

> "From everyone who has been given much, much will be demanded; and from the one who has been entrusted with much, much more will be asked." (Luke 12:48)

To whom much is given, much is required. That is the message. Paul believed he had been given much, and he believed he needed to use it for the glory of God. Humility means thanking God for his gifts, and then getting busy using them.

Some of you reading this have been given gifts, and you are, with false humility, saying, "Oh, no, I don't think I can do that." Is that any different from the wicked servant who buried his talent of money in the ground? (Matthew 25:18). Outwardly, that man may have seemed to be humble and self-effacing. He was not. Jesus found him to be disgusting. Jesus never used the word "wicked" lightly. Humility in his case would have meant embracing responsibility, not hiding what had been given. Some of us need to hear this message. Do you embrace your gifts and the responsibility they bring, or do you cover them and pretend they are not there?

What Humility Will Mean

As we have seen, humility and gratitude are twin virtues. The humble heart always thanks God for what has so generously been given. The humble heart further trusts God, believing that he knew what he was doing when he gave this talent or that talent. When I was in my early days of preaching, people would compliment my sermons. It was not uncommon for me to downplay their affirmation and say something like, "Thanks, but it could have been a lot better." This continued until my young bride finally told me that I was insulting people's intelligence. I was basically saying, "Thanks, but no thanks, because I know you aren't really a good judge of these things." I guess I thought I was being humble. Humility encourages good-hearted people, but I don't think my comments encouraged anyone. Later, even when I felt I could have done better, I learned to appreciate what God was still doing through my weakness. I learned to accept the talent I had and to praise God that someone felt edified or built-up by it.

What about the person who believes he has a gift that he really doesn't have? And there are several such people. This need not be a long-standing problem. Let these people try their "talent," and if they are truly humble, they will ask someone else for confirmation of it. If they don't have that talent, they will learn quickly. Such a one may want to get a second opinion before he draws definite conclusions because any one person can be wrong about such things. The prideful person, however, will not ask for evaluation. He either fears rejection, or he is just so sure he sees himself better than anyone else does. To use the language from my childhood, such a person "needs a good talkin' to." If he is willing to repent and be humble, he can learn what talent he does not have and move on to finding what he does have.

Humility starts with gratitude for our talents, but it moves on to gratitude for the talents of others. Humility recognizes that no one has all the talents. John over here may be exceptional in one area, but he needs to remember others may be much stronger in another area. Or John may need to see that his great talent could never have been maximized without the help of *a collection of people* who are individually less talented.

A while back some friends got tickets for my wife and me for the Boston Symphony summer performance at the famous Tanglewood. That particular night we heard one of the greatest cellists in the world. Hardly knowing a cello from an oboe, I was, nevertheless, ready to buy his CD in the little store after the performance. But how good would his presentation have been without a whole host of lesser-known musicians, under the direction of a capable conductor? The humble man or woman recognizes not only that his talent is a gift, but that it is a gift that thrives in the context of others and their talents. Simply put, the humble heart keeps saying, "I need others."

Paul's teaching in 1 Corinthians 12 was designed to put an end to all prideful attitudes regarding some gift or talent (and such attitudes were not in short supply in Corinth!):

> The body is a unit, though it is made up of many parts; and though all its parts are many, they form one body. So it is with Christ. (1 Corinthians 12:12)

The church, Paul said, is a body composed of many parts. All these parts together form something powerful and significant, but no part on its own is valuable and useful without the others. The greatest leader will do nothing without others to lead and others with various talents to support, refine and magnify his talent.

> If the whole body were an eye, where would the sense of hearing be? If the whole body were an ear, where would the sense of smell be? (1 Corinthians 12:17)

If anyone is tempted (and surely someone will be) to look at the talents of others and think, "That is what I would like to have," they must remember the incredible need there is for diversity. They must never think that any one talent is "the" talent to have. In the same way no individual should think that his talent is a more godly one or more useful one than someone else's. The gift giver gave a variety of talents—all of them needed. Humility confesses that God knew exactly what he was doing.

Perhaps you are reading this and you think of someone with obvious speaking or singing skills. Perhaps you look at your life and cannot identify any great talent that you have. Watch out for pride coming in the back door. Pride can arise over what we do not have just as it can arise over what we do have. You can be sure that you have a role. Humility before God submits to the role he has designed for you.

I know a woman who has many limitations and numerous health problems. She is in a wheelchair. She has little formal education. She would not be highly regarded by talent scouts. But she has recognized that she has a gift of encouragement, and she has cultivated that gift. She has become known as a prayer warrior. She writes letters to Christians around the world. She corresponds with key leaders. Her encouragement of others has almost become legendary. She is grateful to be in the church, not bitter about her circumstances, and she is determined that she will let God use her in any way that he pleases. She is a humble disciple of Jesus.

Before we leave the subject of humility and talent, let me warn you about one other sneaky way that pride sometimes shows up in our hearts. Perhaps you do not boast about your talent or try to push it on others. On the other hand, being quietly confident about what you have, you do not hide it in the ground either, but you try to use it as God intends. But something goes wrong, terribly wrong: Others don't seem to recognize what you can do, and you get passed over when it comes to many opportunities. You may see younger people or those who have been Christians a shorter time than you being given a chance to do something when you are not. At such a time, pride often rears its ugly head and then turns into the two-headed monster—named bitter envy.

When such a temptation comes, I know of no better statement than the one made by John the Baptist: "A man can receive only what is given him from heaven" (John 3:27). John's disciples were concerned that so many people were going to Jesus instead of John. The newcomer was getting more attention than the veteran, and they did not think it was good or fair. John's statement cuts two ways. When I am tempted with pride, bitterness and envy, I need to understand that when it is time for me to receive something, God will make it happen. On the other hand, I need to see that if someone else is receiving an opportunity, it is because God decided it was time. In either case, bitterness and envy grow from pride that believes we know better than God knows or doubts that God is really in control. Too many talented and useful Christians are stewing because they feel overlooked, and the church is losing out. Sure, be honest with someone. Bring your feelings out in the open, but then hear the counsel of John the Baptist.

Pride often shows up in connection with talent. We must remind ourselves of the truth (about where our talent came from) and confess our pride quickly. When you are praised for something you have done, be grateful that God has used you, and thank him for his grace. Know that without his gift, his free gift, it would not have happened. Never downplay good that is done for that would minimize the work of the Spirit. Rejoice in the good and clearly, firmly and with conviction give the glory—all of it—to God.

• **Thought Question** •

How does humility free you to use your talents in the best way?

the conclusion

chapter 19

the pursuit of humility

Writing a book about humility has been a daunting task. There is no shortage of scriptural sources or examples. However, I have had to face my fear that for the rest of my life, I will be challenged by my own words. But so be it.

My goal is put forth by the apostle Paul in Ephesians 4:2: "Be *completely* humble and gentle..." (emphasis added). Not just humble—completely humble. In view of that statement we all have much more progress to make, and that means all of us need to make the pursuit of humility a serious priority. Humility is so contrary to our nature that we will not have it without a passionate desire for it.

Paul tells the Colossian Christians,

> Therefore, as God's chosen people, holy and dearly loved, *clothe yourselves* with compassion, kindness, *humility,* gentleness and patience. (Colossians 3:12, emphasis added)

To walk out of our rooms or homes without first clothing ourselves with humility is to walk out spiritually naked. A leader who walks into a meeting without humility is spiritually naked. The disciple of Jesus who tries to share his faith without humility is spiritually naked. As in the fairy tale, everyone sees it as it is, and someone inevitably will shout out, "The emperor has no clothes!"

No one gets into the wedding banquet of the kingdom unless properly clothed (Matthew 22:11-13). And that clothing includes humility, not a necklace of pride (Psalm 73:6). Let's look more closely at the idea of being clothed with humility by considering the garments of the humble.

A Towel

First, put on a towel. In this book you have read several references to the Savior who came with a towel. Jesus was among us as one who served.

> So he got up from the meal, took off his outer clothing, and wrapped a towel around his waist. After that, he poured water into a basin and began to wash his disciples' feet, drying them with the towel that was wrapped around him....
> "Now that I, your Lord and Teacher, have washed your feet, you also should wash one another's feet." (John 13:4, 5, 14)

Are we eager to become more humble? Not unless we are also eager to serve. We are never so important that we don't need to serve in the mundane ways. How serious can we be about the pursuit of humility if we avoid the towel, the dirty work, the tasks of the housekeeper or the orderly? Yes, it is true. Jesus did not mean we must literally wash feet. But he did mean something with this command—something humbling. If we think we are too important for such things, we are far from the kingdom.

Clothing of the Groomsmen

Second, put on the clothing of the groomsmen. When the word reached John the Baptist of Jesus' success, John probably dismayed his competitive followers with these words:

> "The friend who attends the bridegroom waits and listens for him, and is full of joy when he hears the bridegroom's voice. That joy is mine, and it is now complete. He must become greater; I must become less." (John 3:29b-30)

This amazing attitude needs to characterize us all. We must be happy that others become greater if the gosel is advanced.

The apostle Paul instructs the Philippian church (especially Euodia and Syntyche who did not have this attitude—Philippians 4:2) to put others' interests above their own:

> Do nothing out of selfish ambition or vain conceit, but in *humility consider others better than yourselves.* Each of you should look not only to your own interests, but also to the interests of others. (Philippians 2:3-4, emphasis added)

To pursue humility, we must recognize the enemy: selfish ambition. This helps us to concentrate on its opposite, the success of others. Selfish ambition has nothing to do with Jesus Christ. There was not an ounce of it in him. Nothing moves people more than those who selflessly support others for success. As pride tears down a house, so humbly desiring the best for our fellow Christians builds a house that lasts. Whatever leadership position we find ourselves in, what is required is a humble spirit that seeks what is best for others. We are at our finest, not when we excel personally, but when we help others to excel and shine.

Sackcloth

Third, we will need to clothe ourselves with sackcloth. Frequently, in the Old Testament we find sackcloth to be the clothing of choice when it was time to express contrition and brokenness over sin. Typical is this passage from Nehemiah:

> On the twenty-fourth day of the same month, the Israelites gathered together, fasting and wearing sackcloth and having dust on their heads. Those of Israelite descent had separated themselves from all foreigners. They stood in their places and confessed their sins and the wickedness of their fathers. (Nehemiah 9:1-2)

Proud people will stop talking about sin. They will make excuses. They will become skillful at rationalization. The humble man takes sin seriously. He realizes how it offends a holy God.

He faces the fact that it hurts others in his life, and he deals with his sin with godly sorrow. If we would pursue humility, we must first be honest about our sin and then broken and contrite over it. Those who think they have become too mature for such a response are completely deceived. How many marriages could be transformed if husbands and wives could learn to don the sackcloth. How much unity could be restored among believers if sackcloth were brought back into style.

Our friend Gordon Ferguson is a highly respected teacher and author. But the more important thing about him is that he has a reputation for being open about his life. Because of this, he is often affirmed for his humility. He responds, "I don't confess my sin because I am so humble. I do it because it helps me to be humble." Sure, it takes a certain degree of humility to put on the sackcloth in the first place, but to be seen in such a state of brokenness and need greatly aids the pursuit of humility. It is hard to look down on those to whom you have just confessed your sin. And when you have been that open, others will find you easy to approach.

Salvation

Fourth, nothing is so humbling as to remember the source of salvation. Our deliverance, our redemption, our glory and our victory have all come from God. Isaiah describes those who are clothed by God's grace:

> I delight greatly in the Lord;
> > my soul rejoices in my God.
> For he has clothed me with garments of salvation
> > and arrayed me in a robe of righteousness,
> as a bridegroom adorns his head like a priest,
> > and as a bride adorns herself with her jewels.
> > (Isaiah 61:10)

We need to wear our garments of salvation and let everyone know where we got them. They were a free gift. If we would pursue humility, we must deliberately remind ourselves of where we came from and who brought us to where we are today. Paul, at the end of his life and missionary journeys, writes:

> Here is a trustworthy saying that deserves full acceptance: Christ Jesus came into the world to save sinners—of whom I am the worst. (1 Timothy 1:15)

> For I am the least of the apostles and do not even deserve to be called an apostle, because I persecuted the church of God. (1 Corinthians 15:9)

Paul's usage of the present tense, "I am," demonstrates his constant awareness that he is what he is by the grace of God. If Paul is still conscious of this at the end of many years of selfless service, how much more do we need to be aware that we are sinners daily in need of forgiveness? It removes that edge of self-righteousness and enables us to be content and relaxed and giving to all others. We were sinners, we are forgiven sinners, and we will be forgiven sinners until God takes us home to heaven. If we forget that, we forget the very basis of our position with God.

> Search me, O God, and know my heart;
>   test me and know my anxious thoughts.
> See if there is any offensive way in me,
>   and lead me in the way everlasting.
> (Psalm 139:23-24)

David's prayer is the right one for us as we pursue humility. "Show me, O God, when my heart grows proud. Give me the tests that will reveal to me my pride and my arrogance. Put people in my life who will tell me the truth. Please, do not let me be deceived." We must stop thinking that we have an excuse because "everyone is prideful." We must no longer smile at qualities that make heaven shudder. We must not overlook pride just because the bottom line looks good. God will either lift us up or bring us down, based on the quality of our heart.

In the fairy tale the emperor runs off embarrassed by the youth who yells out the truth about his nakedness. God forbid that it is Jesus, our King, who tells us of our unholy apparel at the gates of heaven! Pursue humility. Clothe yourself with humility. Don't leave home without it!

▪ Thought Question ▪

Which of the four items of clothing do you most need to put on in your pursuit of humility?

chapter 20

the power of humility

The most important question we can ask about anything is, "Does it please God?" Humility always passes that test and, for that reason, would be the right thing for our lives, whatever else we might say about it.

However, humility not only pleases God, but humility is powerful. Men and women who learn humility will experience victories and will see results that will never be present in the lives of prideful souls.

Prideful men and women are often powerful in a worldly sense, but their lives are devoid of spiritual and relational victory. One does not have to be humble to accumulate wealth, be successful in business, achieve political influence or be known for academic excellence. Prideful souls function quite well in all these and other arenas. But it is most common to find prideful people who have gained worldly success but have no clue about how to be happily married, how to be close to their children or how to have lasting friendships. They certainly have no walk with God.

The prideful soul can be successful—at all the things that ultimately do not matter. He will have no success where it really counts. What is missing in his life is the power of humility.

Humility should be our goal, whatever the apparent results, but the fact is that the results are dramatic. While humility sounds like an anemic word to some, in reality it unleashes divine power that can raise us to life on a new and higher plane.

God's Favor

First and foremost, humility is powerful because it brings to your life the favor of God. "God gives grace to the humble." That is the theme of this book. God is not detached and uninvolved in the lives of people. He is frequently described in the Scriptures as the God who wants to bless, and there is absolutely nothing that can stop him from blessing those with humble hearts.

When someone finds favor in the eyes of God, the things that really matter in his life will all be better. He will not have the finest car. She will not live in the biggest house. He will not be the most popular performer. She will not be the biggest vote-getter. But when someone finds favor in God's eyes, the things that count the most will be there in ever-increasing fashion. Humility will never mean an absence of problems. It will not mean comfort and ease, but it will bring an assortment of circumstances and experiences that God will blend together to make life rich and full of depth and meaning.

The Psalmist well understood how important it is to receive God's blessing, when he wrote:

> May the favor of the Lord our God rest upon us;
> establish the work of our hands for us—
> yes, establish the work of our hands. (Psalm 90:17)

Our greatest need is our need for God. We need his work on our behalf. We work, but we need him to "establish the work of our hands." We need him to take our efforts and then make them all they can be.

Life is far too complex and unpredictable for us to figure it out or to be able to manage it on our own. The humble soul deeply believes this. We need God shining his face on us, holding us in the palm of his hand, gently leading and guiding us. We need him to give us grace and to work in unseen ways behind the scenes for our good in all things. We need God to protect us and keep us safe.

Those who find this repugnant do so because they are prideful souls, unwilling to admit who man is and who God is. However, no disdain for these ideas changes the nature of reality. If you do not like it that you need air or water, what you like or do not like changes nothing. The same is true in relation to God: We need him. We need his blessing and his favor. Without those things from him, we miss what is most crucial in life.

Humility is powerful, above all, because it gets the attention of God. God is drawn to the humble heart. His radar picks up humility immediately. His squadrons of grace fly quickly and release their payloads of mercy on the lives of those with humble hearts. Show me a humble heart, and I will show you a person amazed at the way God has worked in his or her life. You will look at these people's lives and you will, of course, see that they have had trials, but you will see a peace in their eyes that says, "Yes, but God worked powerfully in all of these things." They will not be trying to *look* spiritual as they say this; they will be deeply convinced of it. They will be standing in awe of the difference God has made in their lives.

Humility is the most powerful attitude that can exist in the human heart because nothing else so brings to your life the might and power of the Almighty God.

Personal Growth

Nothing is really powerful, from a spiritual perspective, unless it changes people. The power of humility is seen in the way it brings change to every heart and every life in which it is found. Humble people are always changing. Their humility creates fertile ground in which growth thrives.

As the two of us writing this book look at our years of ministry, counseling and shepherding, we think of people who have changed dramatically. Without exception these were people who demonstrated humility. Prideful people do sometimes change, but not in ways that are righteous. What happens quickly with the humble does not happen at all with the prideful. This is unbreakable spiritual law. The two of us look at those times in our personal lives when change was the greatest and those times when change seemed to stop. Once again, we see clearly that there has always been a correlation between humility and growth, and a corresponding correlation between pride and stagnation.

Why did the Ethiopian in Acts 8 change? Because he was humble. Why did Saul of Tarsus undergo one of the most dramatic life changes in history? Because he was finally humbled. Why did a tough jailer in Philippi become a totally new man? Because he was humbled by his situation and by the word of God.

I remember one year in my life in which I probably changed more than any other. It all happened because of a specific decision I made to humble myself before God and before other spiritual people. I had gone through a year of diminishing spiritual strength. I was sinking deep into a pit where I was filled with negativity and discontentment. Pride had taken over in many areas of my life. Nothing in me was changing for the better. But when I humbled myself and very quickly became open about my life, I was amazed at how each day seemed to bring a fresh insight and growth. Others who knew me well were frequently commenting about changes that they saw in me. In the church atmosphere that I was in at the time, there were some tradition-bound souls who did not like the changes, but there was no doubt that they saw them.

From year 1 when I was not changing, to year 2 when I was, God had not changed. The Bible had not changed. My responsibilities had not changed. So what was different? My heart. Year 1: proud. Year 2: humble. Year 1: defensive about my life and my ministry. Year 2: eager to learn from others and quick to confess my sin. The power of humility was evident. I am deeply grateful for the events of that year and how God worked to humble me. It was in that year, now more than twenty years ago, that my convictions about the power of humility began to develop.

How much are you changing? Maybe you have blamed your lack of growth on a variety factors. There is one fundamental reason it does not happen: a lack of humility. Humility is powerful because humility will always bring change.

Unity

What people can achieve when they are united is remarkable. Unity is powerful. An army that is united can often defeat an opponent with superior skills when the opponent is plagued by division. The wise man certainly had it right when he said:

> Though one may be overpowered,
>   two can defend themselves.
> A cord of three strands is not quickly broken.
> (Ecclesiastes 4:12)

Two people united can make a difference. Three people united will be hard to stop. A community of people united is a force to be reckoned with. A worldwide movement of Christians who are united will turn the world upside down (or right side up!). Unity is powerful, and whatever produces unity is powerful. It is no accident that when Paul charges the Ephesians to "make every effort to keep the unity of the Spirit" that the verse preceding that one calls us to "be completely humble" (Ephesians 4:2-3). Humility is essential to unity.

Put a group of people in a room, and let them start to work on a problem. The first thing you will notice is their diversity, not their unity. People see things in very different ways. Opinions are like noses: Everybody has one. When pride rears its ugly head, people will stubbornly hold to their positions, and the result will be a stalemate or paralysis. But if the people in this group are first of all humble before God and humble before his word, and then they are humble in their dealings with one another, their diversity will be transformed into unity. The best ideas from various people will be blended together to produce something better than any one person could have developed.

When they unite behind the group consensus, you have a group ready to make a difference. Humility produces unity in marriages, in families, in churches and in spiritual movements.

I have always been impressed with the humility that characterized the relationship of Jesus and John the Baptist. These two, at the very beginning of the Christian movement, gave us an example that must be imitated. It would be hard to find two men more different in outward style. John arrived on the scene first and attracted great crowds. Jesus would come later and the stage was set for rivalry. But John eliminated the possibility of tension when he said: "After me will come one who is more powerful than I, whose sandals I am not fit to carry" (Matthew 3:11b). With Jesus not yet on the scene, John called people to focus not on himself, but on the one coming later. Humility in action. In another book, I have continued the story:

> But then here comes Jesus, and what is his first move with John? "Then Jesus came from Galilee to be baptized by John" (3:13). Jesus comes out, most likely stands in line with all the others, with the desire to place his body in John's hands for immersion. Humility in action.
> Then John responds. "But John tried to deter him, saying, 'I need to be baptized by you, and do you come to me?'" (3:13-14). Jesus, in so many words, says "This is the right thing. I need to humble myself and submit to your baptism" (3:15a). In humility, John then submitted to Jesus' submission (3:15b). Surely, Satan hated it. These two powerful men just kept humbling themselves before one another, and the bond of unity grew tighter and tighter. Such a pattern continued throughout their lives.*

Whenever you find division in a marriage, in a household, in an office or in a church, you can be sure pride is alive and working. You can be sure that someone or several someones are not willing to humble themselves after the example of Jesus and John. You can be sure that people are much more concerned about holding on to what is theirs than they are about demonstrating humility.

Unity is always achievable, but a price must be paid. We must all take our pride up the hill of Calvary and let it be crucified with Christ. In writing to the Philippian church Paul made the same connection between humility and unity that we saw earlier in Ephesians:

> ...then make my joy complete by being like-minded, having the same love, being one in spirit and purpose. Do nothing out of selfish ambition or vain conceit, but in humility consider others better than yourselves. (Philippians 2:2-3)

Having said this, Paul then calls us to take this to the extreme. He says our attitude should be the same as that of Christ Jesus (v5) and that means going all the way to the cross (v8). When we follow Jesus to Calvary and crucify all our pride, unity will come—we will be one in spirit and in purpose. The process may take some time, but we will get there.

Division has always been Satan's primary objective. Humility thwarts his plans, brings about unity and empowers God's people to change their communities and change the world. Humility must be practiced in every relationship and at every level of leadership because it always unleashes God's power.

Final Thoughts

What is a healthy soul? It is one permeated with humility. It is a soul free of pride. Pride is a soul pollutant. Pride prevents the soul from communing with God—the One who gives life and wholeness to the soul. Pride keeps the soul from communing with other souls and stops relationships that give richness to life.

When the soul is humble, it can soar. It can stand in awe of God and see clearly the miracles of his grace. The humble soul is free to be grateful and free to give praise. When the soul is humble, it can hear clearly the voice of God and understand his will. When the soul is humble, it can touch the work of God and become part of a great plan to change many lives. When the soul is humble, it is liberated to accept challenge, and it will eagerly embrace adventure that will advance the kingdom of God.

Quite simply, when the soul is humble, it is emptied of self, and it can be filled with the Spirit of God, the power of God and the wisdom of God.

O God, expose our pride.
Keep us always humble. Amen.

▪ Thought Question ▪

What are your personal convictions about
the power of humility?
How do you let others see those convictions?

NOTES

*"Humility in Action" in *Jesus with the People* (Billerica, Mass: DPl, 1996), 14-16. See this chapter for a more detailed look at the interaction of Jesus and John.

appendixes

appendix 1

is pride ever good?

As we have attempted to show in this book, God consistently calls for humility, and he consistently gives grace to the humble. He just as consistently condemns those with proud hearts—meaning those who are arrogant, independent of him and others, self-centered, boastful or unwilling to listen to advice and input. Such a man is a fool, according to the book of Proverbs. Pride is a deadly sin.

However, thoughtful Bible students will immediately recall several places in Scripture where the word "pride" is used in a different way, in a way in which the meaning is actually positive, from a spiritual perspective. In recent years as scientists have learned more and more about the human body, we have heard them distinguish between "bad cholesterol" and "good cholesterol." They have urged people to learn the difference between these two before they rush to eliminate all cholesterol from their diets. In a similar way we need to learn the difference between "bad pride" and "good pride." This book has focused primarily on the first because the overwhelming theme of Scripture is that pride must die and humility must live. However, we need to say something about the second type of pride.

If you use a concordance or an electronic Bible software program, you will find something very interesting. In the New International Version every use of the word "pride" in the Old Testament is a reference to the "bad pride" we have looked at in this book. However, every use of the word "pride" in the New Testament is a reference to the other type of pride that we are now dubbing the "good pride." This is slightly misleading. It can sound like the Old and New Testaments each have a very different emphasis, but this is not true at all. Instead of using "pride" to describe the bad pride, the New Testament uses the word "proud." The proud heart that we have described in this book is condemned just as forcefully in the New Testament as it is in the Old Testament. Consider just three of many possible examples:

> Live in harmony with one another. Do not be proud, but be willing to associate with people of low position. Do not be conceited. (Romans 12:16)
>
> Love is patient, love is kind. It does not envy, it does not boast, it is not proud. (1 Corinthians 13:4)
>
> But he gives us more grace. That is why Scripture says:
> "God opposes the proud
>   but gives grace to the humble." (James 4:6)

What is the "good pride," and when and how can a Christian have it? Let's look first at the several passages where pride is used in this different way. We would call your attention to three facts: (1) There are very few of these passages (only five, compared to literally hundreds of references in both testaments to the deadly pride that destroys relationships with God and men). (2) With one exception, all of these are from the pen of Paul, and this usage may have been peculiar to his background and training. (3) There is really no command to have this kind of pride. There is no indication that God wills us to have it. Certainly, there is nothing similar to the injunctions to be humble that are found so often. Notice that this is something that one has almost incidentally, without there being anything wrong with it:

> We are not trying to commend ourselves to you again, but are giving you an opportunity to take pride in us, so that you

can answer those who take pride in what is seen rather than in what is in the heart. (2 Corinthians 5:12)

I have great confidence in you; I take great pride in you. I am greatly encouraged; in all our troubles my joy knows no bounds. (2 Corinthians 7:4)

Therefore show these men the proof of your love and the reason for our pride in you, so that the churches can see it. (2 Corinthians 8:24)

Each one should test his own actions. Then he can take pride in himself, without comparing himself to somebody else. (Galatians 6:4)

The brother in humble circumstances ought to take pride in his high position. But the one who is rich should take pride in his low position, because he will pass away like a wild flower. (James 1:9-10)

The American Heritage Dictionary gives as one of the definitions for pride: "pleasure or satisfaction taken in an achievement, a possession, or an association." An English dictionary is not always a good guide to understanding Biblical words, but this is exactly the way the word "pride" is used in these cases. Paul is getting satisfaction from seeing those to whom he has reached out growing and changing in Christ. The reference in Galatians, similarly, is to having the satisfaction that comes from seeing what you have been able to do by the power of God's Spirit (as opposed to what you have done by your own power, Galatians 3:3), without the need to make someone else look less. Certainly, there is no hint here of destructive pride. One only needs to look at Galatians 6:3 to see this very clearly: "If anyone thinks he is something when he is nothing, he deceives himself." Another passage in the same context is significant: "Let us not become conceited, provoking and envying each other" (Galatians 5:26).

James, in the same way, in his letter talks about how one gets satisfaction. He teaches that we can learn to get it in a totally different manner from what is normal. The Christian who has little can get satisfaction from the fact that his position in God's economy may very well be a "high position." The Christian who has much materially (and James may be speaking a bit with tongue in cheek here) should find satisfaction in his coming to the "low position" of humility in Christ, realizing that all the trappings that belong to the world's high positions will pass away like the wildflowers.

With these things in mind, how might Christians today take pride in something? Consider several examples:

- You share your faith with the neighbors next door and see them come to Christ. As you further help them and see their marriage change and their children change, you take pride in their lives—that is, you get a great deal of satisfaction from seeing God use you to help bring this about. That is very different from being boastful about the fact that you did it or from putting someone else down because they have not done what you have done.

- You raise your children to be Christians. You look forward to the day when they will stand before others and declare, "Jesus is Lord!" When the day finally comes, you are beaming. You are smiling from sea to shining sea! You are taking great pride in this tremendous event. You feel tremendous pleasure and satisfaction. You give glory to God, for you know that he made it happen, and at the same time you feel a great sense of personal accomplishment.

- You are a single mom with two kids. You work a full-time job, but you work another job at home, meeting their needs and discipling their characters. They finish high school and go on to college or productive work. They become responsible adults who love God and bring others to him. You look at those pictures on the refrigerator and in the bedroom and in the living room and in the hall, and you beam! You take pride in those two kids and in what they have done against some tough odds.

- You are a physically challenged Christian. You have dealt with a disability all your life, but you have never given in or given up. You became a disciple of Jesus and you learned new spiritual skills that helped you to overcome. You finished college, landed a good job and became a productive member of God's church. You have every reason to feel good about what God has taught you, what God has helped you to become, and about how God has used you. As long as you keep your eyes on God and do not become boastful or arrogant, you can take pride in what has happened.

On we could go with more examples, but hopefully, the point is clear: This type of pride bears no resemblance to the pride we have focused on in this book. There is not one thing in these passages that would water down or dilute anything that has been said about the need to crucify our pride so that true and complete humility can be resurrected. There is nothing here to cause us to say, "Well, maybe pride is not so bad." The stubborn, arrogant, headstrong, conceited, independent or defensive spirit is always wrong.

Let us take great satisfaction in what God accomplishes through us. Let us beam and shine and feel good. But let us give all the glory to God!

appendix 2

classic expressions of pride

1. Not wanting to talk with someone or spend time with someone because they just don't quite measure up.

2. Thinking: "They should have asked me to do that. I would have done it better."

3. Wanting to turn the conversation to highlight something you have done.

4. Getting most of your sense of worth from having a group of people who are loyal to you.

5. Feeling a good report of someone else lessens your worth.

6. Having as your deepest conviction about advice that, "After all, advice is just advice. You don't have to take it."

7. Lack of openness about important areas of your life like your times with God, your marriage, your dating, your other relationships.

8. Asking your spouse not to discuss your marriage with others or to call for help.

9. Not asking for counsel, advice or perspective about dating, marriage, parenting, finances, evangelism and other vital areas.

10. Knowing that you are wrong, but resisting admitting it to yourself and then to others.

11. For men only: being particularly defensive about something pointed out to you by a woman.

12. For leaders: preaching what others ought to be doing, but not being open about the fact that you are not doing those things.

13. Believing your approach to ministry is much better than that of others. Thinking you have a right balance or emphasis that others don't have.

14. Hearing about some leader's problems and feeling better about yourself because that has not happened to you.

15. Hearing a speaker giving out praise and waiting for your name to be spoken.

16. Feeling cheated because you did not get to work with someone or did not get to be involved with a project for which you thought you were well-suited.

17. Only half listening to what someone is telling you because they are not that important a person.

18. Resenting the input of a much younger Christian. Feeling that they should not give such to someone who has been around as long as you. (Thinking longevity gives you some exemptions.)

19. Being given a lot to do and then going after it, without much prayer.

20. Seldom asking others seriously to pray for you.

21. Not volunteering for something because you fear making mistakes or failing, and don't want to look bad.

22. Not being supportive and encouraging of peers. Not celebrating their victories because you are highly competitive.

23. Interrupting and finishing people's sentences.

24. Having a strong desire to guard your territory and letting that rob you of a greater "good of the church" outlook.

25. Filtering out things that you don't like to hear from the advice and counsel you are given. Doing only those elements that you already felt good about.

26. Avoiding situations where you might have to do something that looks menial or servile. Coming up with great spiritual excuses about it.

27. Consistently thinking that the assignments given you or the ministry arrangements made for you don't show appreciation for who you are and what you have to offer.

28. Listening to advice, agreeing with advice, but then not putting it into practice.

29. Neglecting to pray when giving and taking advice from other Christians.

30. Not planning special times to just go be with God.

31. Thinking pride is not that big a problem for you.

32. Not confessing sin unless you are backed into a corner and confronted.

appendix 3

short thoughts on humility

- The deepest humility comes from contemplating the greatness of God. Humility from any other source is shallow and vulnerable.

- Jesus was humble even before he entered into this world. Without humility he would not have come.

- Jesus' coming means that the powerful God of the universe is, in his essence, humble.

- If there is not much that awes you, pride rules in your heart.

- The humble man will be an approachable man. When people are afraid of others, pride is usually involved. Jesus was the perfect Son of God. But he was famously approachable.

- We need to confess our sin not because we *are* humble but *to keep* us humble.

- Humility is not low self-esteem. You can have low self-esteem and also be extremely prideful.

- The humble person sees his weaknesses. He can tell you what they are because he has asked others to help him see them.

- Humility means having a willingness to associate with (have friendships with) those of low position (in the world's eyes). It further means not viewing people of lower position as lower at all.

- The humble man puts his confidence in God, not in his ability or talent.

- The humble man considers the words of his critics. He knows they may be wrong. But he recognizes that they can be right.

- The humble man is not afraid to look needy. (In other words, he is not afraid to admit the truth!)

- The humble man sees the impact of others on his life, and he is grateful and appreciative.

- The humble man is not just willing to confess his sin; he is known for confessing his sin.

- The humble man is not completely free of pride. He is one who quickly sees his pride and repents.

- Humility is like perfection: It is a goal to be pursued, even as we confess freely that we have not arrived.

- The power of humility does not lie in the attaining of it but in the pursuit of it.

- The humble man listens well when others speak. The prideful man does not think he needs to.

- The humble man listens well to all people. The prideful man selects those who deserve his attention.

- The humble man is willing to be embarrassed if it might advance the gospel. The prideful man must protect his image.

- The humble man will often see the need for prayer. He will be known for his prayer life.

- The humble person is always a grateful person. Ingratitude springs from pride and self-absorption—from a view that says, "I deserve better."

- "I deserve" is not in the vocabulary of the humble. "I am blessed" is what comes out of his mouth, for that is what is in his heart.

- The humble person freely, joyfully and thankfully accepts forgiveness. Pride is what causes one to say, "Oh, no, I couldn't."

- Nothing should humble us more than the cross of Christ. If we can stand in the presence of such unconditional love and not be brought to our knees, our hearts have grown rock hard.

- How can we stand at the foot of the cross and look down on anyone? Are we forgetting that we put Jesus there and that he was dying for us?

- Humility is not about being a nice person. It is about unleashing the power of God.

- The prideful man is wise in his own eyes and clever in his own sight. The Bible says "woe" to such a man (Isaiah 5:21).

- Want to see a man humbled because he has seen God? Read Isaiah 6 and Revelation 1:9-17.

- Isaiah went on to be a powerful prophet. John wrote a powerful book. It all started in complete humility. It always does.

- "To keep me from becoming conceited…" (2 Corinthians 12:7): God is concerned about keeping his people from becoming conceited and prideful. He will do whatever it takes.

- People who have not stood in awe of God are not ready to serve God. A man who goes forth to serve God or to lead the people of God is a dangerous man if he has not and does not regularly stand in awe of God.

- Pride wants credit. Humility wants to give it.

www.ingramcontent.com/pod-product-compliance
Lightning Source LLC
Chambersburg PA
CBHW030329100526
44592CB00010B/627